THE LEGEND OF
INGERSOLL-RAND

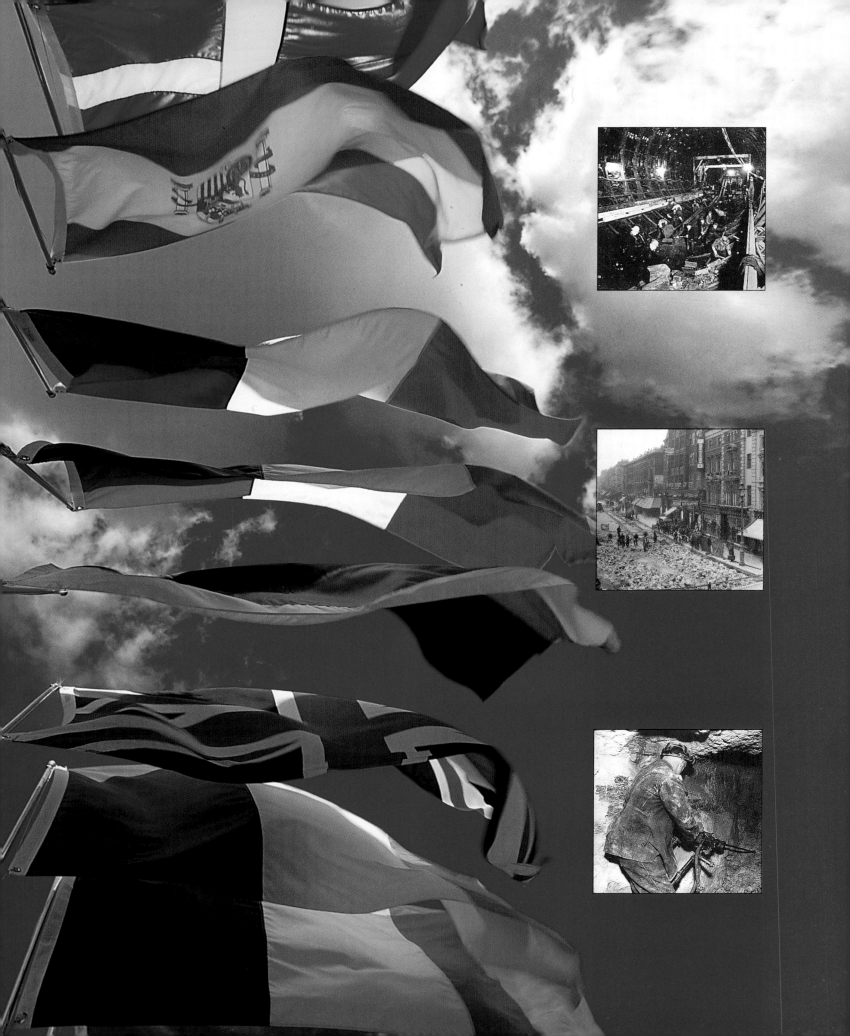

THE LEGEND OF

INGERSOLL-RAND

JEFFREY L. RODENGEN

For Jim
Everyone needs a big brother to lean on...

Also by Jeff Rodengen

The Legend of Chris-Craft

IRON FIST: *The Lives of Carl Kiekhaefer*

Evinrude-Johnson and The Legend of OMC

Serving The Silent Service: The Legend of Electric Boat

The Legend of Honeywell

The Legend of Dr Pepper/Seven Up

The Legend of Briggs & Stratton

The Legend of The Stanley Works

WRITE STUFF SYNDICATE

Write Stuff Syndicate, Inc.

1515 Southeast 4th Avenue
Fort Lauderdale, FL 33316
1-800-900-Book
(1-800-900-2665)
(305) 462-6657

Library of Congress Catalog Card Number
95-060794

ISBN 0-945903-08-1

Completely produced in the United States of America

10 9 8 7 6 5 4 3 2 1

TABLE OF CONTENTS

FOREWORD

by

J. Peter Grace

THERE HAS been a member of the Grace family associated with Ingersoll-Rand for over a century. Ever since my grandfather, William Russell Grace, began acquiring shares in Ingersoll-Sergeant Drill Company in the late 1880s, a member of my family has served as either a senior executive, or as a member of the board. In 1894, W.R. Grace became president of the growing company, setting the stage for the merger in 1905 with the Rand Drill Company, creating Ingersoll-Rand.

My grandfather, whom I never knew as he died nine years before I was born, was a tremendous judge of people. Among his many business talents was the ability, during the most brief of encounters, to identify talent and promise in the people he met. In 1881, he was a director of the Brooklyn Terminal warehouse, one of the largest customers for the W.R. Grace & Company. One day, a young, 15-year-old messenger from the warehouse brought a packet of documents for my grandfather to sign. Grandfather was immediately impressed by the young lad, and observed him closely for the few minutes they were togeth-er. He then asked the messenger to wait outside, and my grandfather phoned the president of the warehouse company. He asked the president for permission to hire the young messenger. Feeling unable to refuse the modest request of his largest client, the warehouse president agreed. The young man, George Doubleday, was hired on the spot. Under the tutelage of my grandfather and his organization, Doubleday learned the skills of business well. Doubleday became president of Ingersoll-Rand from 1913 to 1936, and remained active on the board until 1955 at the age of eighty-nine. That's a remarkable seventy-four years of service to Ingersoll- Rand, and thanks to the sharp eye of W.R. Grace.

My father, J.P. Grace was named vice president of the Ingersoll-Rand Company in 1905, and my uncle, Russell Grace, was made the treasurer. My earliest recollection of the company was being taken around the factory as a child by my uncle, who had three daughters and sort of adopted me as a son. I remember him spending 80 percent of his time telling me how much better Ingersoll-

Rand was being run than W.R. Grace. I was grateful for his friendship, and I learned a great deal from my uncle. He had the ability to see opportunities where others didn't, and he had the guts to pursue them.

Myself, I became president of W.R. Grace at the age of 32, and was elected to the board of Ingersoll-Rand in 1945. I guess I've been on the board for about 50 years now, a long time. Today, I'm considered the member emeritus, but I still attend every meeting, and am still very interested in the great progress that the corporation continues to make throughout the world.

One of the main things that has always impressed me about Ingersoll-Rand is the fact that the vast majority of its leadership has worked its way up through the ranks, having experienced a wide range of responsibilities before taking the reins. This has produced a long line of very balanced, capable and dedicated leadership that has remained loyal to the cause of making Ingersoll-Rand one of the most highly respected enterprises in the world.

Another interesting side of the Ingersoll-Rand story has been the inventive and colorful salesmen, engineers and managers that have been dispatched to nearly every corner of the globe. Their hard work and commitment to helping their customers solve problems have spawned stories that have become legendary from the silver mines on the slopes of Bolivia to the board rooms of America's largest utility companies. Though many of the stories you will read will be entertaining, they all underscore the belief by generations of Ingersoll-Rand employees that "make it right, make it last" has also made generations of Ingersoll-Rand customers very happy.

As I reflect on over a half-century of association with this great company, I'm proud to be part of the 110-year relationship between the Grace family and Ingersoll-Rand.

On the occasion of Ingersoll-Rand's 100th anniversary, author George Koether reflected on the uncommon qualities of two men who helped make the company great -- W.R. Grace and Michael P. Grace,

"They are extraordinary men. It is to their uncommon qualities of inventiveness, enterprise, courage and persistence that Ingersoll-Rand can attribute the strength and breadth of its beginnings and its growth ... We can see the caliber and character of human striving and spirit that are required to build a great enterprise."

AUTHOR'S NOTE

Shortly after completing the foreword to *The Legend of Ingersoll-Rand*, J. Peter Grace succumbed to illness and passed away on April 19, 1995, at the age of 81. Grace served as chief executive of W.R. Grace for 47 years, a term longer than that of any other CEO of a major American company. In 1962, Grace was named by President John F. Kennedy to head a committee promoting U.S. investment in Latin America. In 1982, he was named by President Ronald Reagan as chairman of the Private Sector Survey on Cost Control, which was later named the Grace Commission. His many contributions to both American industry and society would fill many volumes.

It is the first time in over a century that a member of the Grace family has not been represented on the Board.

INTRODUCTION

IT'S NOT OFTEN that the story of an American company is intertwined with industrial development around the world. Ingersoll-Rand is such a company.

The largest and most important structures on the planet have been shaped by Ingersoll-Rand products, from the Panama Canal to the largest hydroelectric facility in the world, the Three Gorges Dam Project currently under construction on China's Yangtze River. Ingersoll-Rand machines have made it possible to shape mountains, carve roads and search for precious resources as no other company has done.

Perhaps the most commonly-known Ingersoll-Rand products are the Jackhamer drill, patented in 1912, and Schlage Locks, produced by a company that Ingersoll-Rand acquired in 1974. But Ingersoll-Rand products are as close as the needle bearings in your automobile, or at work on the roads under construction in your neighborhood.

Roads, train tracks and airports around the world are built with Ingersoll-Rand drills, compactors and air compressors. Coal, oil and water are reached and transported for conversion into energy by Ingersoll-Rand machines. Ingersoll-Rand tools and automated machinery help build automobiles, and bearings produced by the Torrington subsidiary keep them running smoothly.

President, Chairman and Chief Executive Officer James E. Perrella noted that Ingersoll-Rand products are involved in every part of life. "Our products contribute to economic and social progress everywhere," he said in a recent interview. "We think we have a major impact on improving life for everyone."

Ingersoll-Rand products also save lives. When a South African mine collapsed in 1991, an Ingersoll-Rand rescue drill saved 26 miners in record time. When the Chicago River overflowed in 1992, the City of Chicago relied on Ingersoll-Rand pumps, portable generators, air compressors and light towers to help restore and clean up the ravaged city. Ingersoll-Rand compressors aid cancer research and provide power for surgical instruments. Schlage locks offer such proven protection that they are even used to secure the White House.

The Ingersoll-Rand Company is much like its machinery: Large and powerful, yet unobtrusive. You don't notice the machine, you notice what it accomplishes. Ingersoll-Rand is not a flashy company. George Doubleday, president from 1913 to 1955, was so modest that he even refused to give his photograph to newspapers. That same dedication to purpose, mixed with a large dose of humility, still characterizes the organization, though today a multibillion dollar global resource.

Ingersoll-Rand executives, most of whom are engineers, have built Ingersoll-Rand into an industrial giant through excellence in equipment, machinery and customer service, never relying on flashy advertising or catchy slogans. "They know the business, Perrella said. "That is one reason why investors can have confidence in our future."

Despite a low public profile, Ingersoll-Rand has been an important global concern almost from the day Simon Ingersoll patented his steam-powered rock drill in 1871. By 1906, the year after the Ingersoll-Sergeant Rock Drill Company merged with the Rand Drill Company, the new company already had five manufacturing plants, 22 domestic branch sales offices, and 18 foreign offices.

Throughout the years, the company has grown, both in size and in reputation, thanks to its unflagging pursuit of new technology, its uncompromising customer service, and its aggressive policy of business acquisition. Ingersoll-Rand has acquired dozens of industry leaders. In 1968, Ingersoll-Rand acquired the Torrington Company, and in 1974, Schlage Locks. In the late eighties, Ingersoll-Rand joined forces with Dresser Industries in two important joint-ventures. In 1986, Dresser-Rand was created through a partnership between the two industrial giants, and in 1991, Ingersoll-Dresser Pump Company was formed through a similar merging of strategic resources. Ingersoll-Rand's most recent purchase, completed in June 1995, was Clark Equipment Company, acquired for $1.46 billion.

Today, this fascinating company has nearly 45,000 employees around the world and combined sales near $5.5 billion. Under Perrella's leadership Ingersoll-Rand is larger and more aggressive than ever, and continues to shape industrial development and progress throughout the world.

"We have a company with tremendous potential because of the kinds of products we have, and because of our participation in the active, growing markets of developing countries," Perrella said. "We have a vision we're working hard on — to really be every customer's partner or supplier of choice by giving outstanding service."

ACKNOWLEDGMENTS

RESEARCHING, WRITING and publishing *The Legend of Ingersoll-Rand* would not have been possible without the cooperation and assistance of hundreds of individuals. The candid insights of Ingersoll-Rand executives, both active and retired, were of particular importance to this project. The author is especially grateful to James E. Perrella, president, chairman and chief executive officer of Ingersoll-Rand, who generously gave many hours of his valuable time.

Dick Johnson, executive director of public affairs, provided constant assistance throughout the lengthy process of manuscript preparation. Stanley M. Parkhill, recently retired editor and publications manager of *Compressed Air Magazine*, Paul Sumner, retired manager of communication services, and Paul A. Dickard, director of public relations, all devoted much-appreciated skill and energy to the project.

Warm gratitude is extended to Thomas A. Holmes, Theodore H. Black and William Wearly, all former chief executives of Ingersoll-Rand, who shared acquisition strategies, leadership philosophies and thoughtful insights with the author.

Critical insights on both the legacy and promises of Ingersoll-Rand were provided by William G. Mulligan, executive vice president; J. Frank Travis, executive vice president; Thomas McBride, senior vice president and chief financial officer; William J. Armstrong, vice president and treasurer; Paul Bergren, vice president in charge of the Air Compressor Group; Frederick W. Hadfield, vice president in charge of the Ingersoll-Dresser Pump Company; Daniel E. Kletter, vice president in charge of China; Patricia Nachtigal, vice president and general counsel; Allen M. Nixon, vice president in charge of the Torrington Division; James R. O'Dell, vice president in charge of technology; R. Barry Uber, vice president in charge of the Construction Equipment Group; Carlo Piva, president of Instrum-Rand; Jean Torfs, president of Ingersoll-Rand France; Steve Doolittle, managing director of sales, service and development engineering for the GHH-Rand joint venture; John Selko, chief of patents; James Lahey, director of the Total Quality Leadership program, Corporate Secretary Ronald G. Heller, Rick Zimmerman, vice president and general manager of the Rock Drill Division,

Carl Nasca, business unit manager in the Rock Drill Division and Director Alexander H. Massad, retired vice president of the Mobil Oil Corporation.

Retired executives and employees gave generously of their time and expertise, including former presidents D. Wayne Hallstein and David C. Garfield; David Lasier, former president of the Door Hardware Group; William Austin, retired vice president of sales for the Air Compressor Group; Joseph A. Wiendl, retired vice president of sales; Robert Popejoy, former vice president of the Compressor Division; Dick Kniffen, retired director of employee relations; King Cunningham, recently retired vice president of international marketing, Skip Remson, retired manager of human resources, Ernie Hinck, recently retired vice president and general manager of the Rock Drill Division, and salesmen Stan Orben and H. Kirk Lewis.

Research Assistant Jennifer Cataliotti sifted through the many thousands of documents that had accumulated during Ingersoll-Rand's 125-year history. Her energy and attention to detail were critical to the success of this project.

Cheerful assistance was also provided by Flo Ochsenfeld, Eileen Gerke and Marilynn Van Ophuijsen, staff assistants for public affairs; Ronald G. Schrein, director of advertising; Gordon W. Stables, director of government affairs and international marketing; Steve Connell, staff editor; Jeffrey W. Corkill, graphics coordinator; Sharyn Weissman, assistant to Ronald Heller; Mark Kist, production manager; and L.L. "Speed" Lauver.

A special debt of gratitude is also owed to C.H. Vivian, editor of *Compressed Air Magazine* from 1932 to 1957. His unpublished research and careful accumulation of records and archives provided valuable detail and depth for this book.

Finally, a very special thanks to the dedicated staff of Write Stuff Syndicate, Inc., especially Executive Assistant Bonnie Bratton, Creative Director Kyle Newton, Graphic Designer Anne Boeckh, Executive Editor Karen Nitkin, Project Analyst Karine N. Rodengen, Logistics Specialist Joe Kenny, Production Manager Sharon Khan, Proofreader Cathy Ritter and Office Mascot Kodak Rodengen.

Simon Ingersoll's rock drill patent of 1871 gave new life to an old industry. Although Ingersoll patented 27 inventions in his lifetime, the rock drill would be the most universally known.

Couch's assistant, J.W. Fowle, was also interested in drills. Fowle patented his own type of rock drill in 1851 and another in 1866. Fowle's designs were important to the progress of the drill, but he did not have the financial resources to manufacture and market them. Charles Burleigh bought Fowle's patents in 1866 and introduced the product to the marketplace. Variations on these percussion, or drop, drills were used extensively until the hammer drill was developed in 1896 and 1897 by J. George Leyner.[2]

Simon Ingersoll

Simon Ingersoll loved to invent things. When he was 12 years old, he built a small steamboat with a boiler fashioned from a large iron cooking pot. As a young man, he invented a self-propelled steam carriage, similar to what eventually would become the automobile. Though not the first to create such a vehicle, he drove it proudly through the streets of Stamford, Connecticut, charging passengers 10¢ for a trip to nearby New Canaan, Connecticut.[3] Ingersoll also invented a gate latch, a spring scale, and a machine that cut and counted the wooden plugs used by shipbuilders.

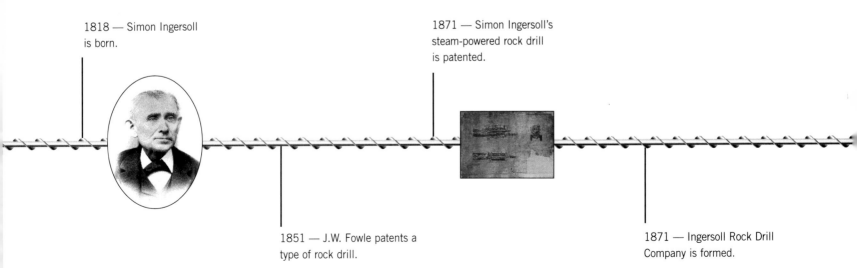

1818 — Simon Ingersoll is born.

1871 — Simon Ingersoll's steam-powered rock drill is patented.

1851 — J.W. Fowle patents a type of rock drill.

1871 — Ingersoll Rock Drill Company is formed.

Born in Connecticut March 3, 1818, Ingersoll married Sarah B. Smith when he was 21 years old. His odd jobs and inventions could not support his young family, which would grow to seven children, so he took up truck gardening. This work entailed growing crops, hauling them to local markets, and selling them. As business grew, he opened a stall in bustling Fulton Market, New York. Sarah died in 1858, and two years later, Simon married Frances Hoyt and had two more children.

One day in the early 1870s, oral tradition suggests, Ingersoll struck up a conversation with John D. Minor, an important New York City contractor. According to *Compressed Air Magazine*, two stories of the historic meeting have survived.

"One story says that Ingersoll, who was always talking about his inventions, struck up

an acquaintance with Minor at his Fulton Street Market. The other account has it that Ingersoll was riding a horse-drawn streetcar in New York one day, carrying a model of his latest invention, apparently on his way to show it to someone whom he hoped to interest. Ingersoll was showing the model to a fellow passenger, when a man across the aisle, who turned out to be Minor, interrupted and asked Ingersoll why he didn't invent something useful. 'Like what, for instance?' asked the surprised Ingersoll. 'A rock drill,' replied Minor."[4]

Minor knew that a mechanical drill would save

Right: This Leyner No. 3 drill was built in 1897. J. George Leyner began designing drills in 1893, and started his own company in 1902. During the years of 1911 and 1912, Ingersoll-Rand acquired the stock of Leyner's company.

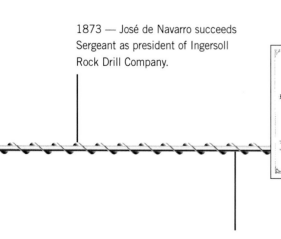

1873 — José de Navarro succeeds Sergeant as president of Ingersoll Rock Drill Company.

1885 — Sergeant Drill Company is formed.

1888 — Ingersoll Rock Drill Company merges with Sergeant Drill Company to form the Ingersoll-Sergeant Drill Company.

1894 — W.R. Grace acquires a controlling share of Ingersoll-Sergeant and becomes president.

machine shop when he was young, and by age 18 he had developed a special machine for making wagon wheel parts. He obtained numerous patents for inventions related to gas regulators, steam pumps, steam boilers, water meters and brickmaking machines.

Sergeant had moved to New York in 1867 and begun work with George Cullingworth in the machine shop at 2nd Avenue and 22nd Street. In 1871, the name of the machine shop was changed from the Hydraulic Machine Company to Sergeant & Cullingworth.

Sergeant refined the Ingersoll drill using valve motion principles borrowed from the Cameron steam pump, manufactured in the same building as Sergeant & Cullingworth. During one of his redesigns, Sergeant created a new valve to improve upon the tappet valve that often needed repair. When the tappet valve broke, pieces went into the cylinder, ruining it. His new drill, popularly known as the Eclipse drill, reduced maintenance and repairs significantly.[15]

Merging Ingersoll and Sergeant

In 1883 or 1884, Sergeant left the Ingersoll Rock Drill Company to try his hand at silver mining. After an unsuccessful venture in Colorado, he returned to the East and started his own company, the Sergeant Drill Company, in 1885. He designed another drill, the Sergeant Auxiliary Valve Drill, which employed both a variable piston stroke and an independent valve. In 1888, the Sergeant Drill Company merged with Ingersoll Rock Drill, forming the Ingersoll-Sergeant Drill Company. The two men primarily responsible for

Stock certificate of the Ingersoll-Sergeant Drill Company, from the late 1890s.

the merger were Robert W. Chapin and Edwin E. Earle, who together secured control of the stock in both companies. Between 1888 and 1891, they sold out. "Earle was the first one affected. His stock, which he owned jointly with his wife and his brother-in-law, was pledged as collateral for a loan that he received from William Russell Grace, head of W.R. Grace & Company."[16]

The Grace Legacy

From 1891 until the death of J. Peter Grace in 1995, there has always been a member of the Grace family in a prominent position at Ingersoll-Rand. William Russell Grace, head of W.R. Grace & Company and owner of Ingersoll-Sergeant stock, was an entrepreneur and adventurer who became the first Irish-born mayor of New York in 1881, serving two nonconsecutive terms. He founded W.R. Grace & Company in Peru in 1854, and quickly established it as the principal shipping and trading company between the Americas. In the 1860s, he established a main branch in New York. In 1880, New York Democrats wanted a mayoral ticket headed by a strong businessman not identified with the corrupt machine politics of Tammany Hall, and persuaded Grace to run.

A tragic event thrust him into the public eye and virtually sealed his victory. On June 28, 1880, while Grace and his family were aboard the *Sewanhaka*, a Long Island commuting steamer, the boiler exploded, igniting a fire. As flames and smoke engulfed the ship, Grace's calm command of the situation saved scores of lives. Of 350 people on the ship, 300 survived the disaster.

> *"Hysterical passengers were jumping from the decks. It takes a cool, strong swimmer to breast the tide and current in that stretch of water. Some managed to make the island, but more were drowned. With the flames roaring nearer, Grace and his wife [Lilius] did what they could to stem the spread of panic and to prevent people from leaping overboard until they were close enough to have a chance in the water. ... The Graces were among the last to jump."*[17]

William Russell Grace, mayor of New York City from 1881 to 1882 and from 1885 to 1886, was president of Ingersoll-Sergeant from 1894 to 1904. His leadership of the company began the legacy of the Grace family relationship with Ingersoll-Rand.

As mayor of New York City, Grace became increasingly interested in his Ingersoll-Sergeant Drill Company stock. New York City was undertaking a remarkable amount of construction, and hundreds of Ingersoll drills were used for the work. W.R. Grace promised himself he would acquire control of the company, and between 1891 and 1897, he nearly tripled his holdings of Ingersoll-Sergeant, increasing his shares from 1,247 to 3,076. By June 1, 1897, the Grace family held 6,177

"[Rand] sold rock drills chiefly to the mining industry, which had to have compressed air to operate drills underground. Ingersoll on the other hand, supplied most of its drills to contractors, who generally used steam for open-air drilling."[10]

Although it is certain that Rand & Waring sold compressors under its name, they were most likely manufactured elsewhere, according to Vivian.

"There is no record of any Rand & Waring factories. If any existed, they would likely have been taken over by the successor firm, Rand Drill Company. We have noted, however, that the latter concern had no compressor factory of its own until it moved to Tarrytown, N.Y. in 1890, and that the compressors that bore its nameplate before that time were built to its specifications by one of four companies in New York. It seems probable that this same arrangement existed under Rand & Waring management."[11]

Whatever their origin, Rand & Waring sold compressors of two different designs in 1878, an L-shaped and a horizontal. In the horizontal variety were a straight-line compressor, a conventional duplex type, and a third, similar to the duplex variety but driven by a poppet-valve engine.

The oldest sales records from Rand Drill indicate that 90 compressors were shipped between

The back cover of a Canadian Rand Drill Company booklet, *Mining Machinery and Equipment.*

1879 and 1882. This steady business prompted Rand to develop additional models. In 1889, the Rand catalog offered four types of air compressors as the standard line, in addition to some special application designs.

Painted Post

Pressed for manufacturing room, the Rand Company in 1899 purchased the Weston Engine Company, in Painted Post, New York.

"The unusual name stems from the custom of Indian chiefs of erecting monuments to celebrate their victories in battle. A tree trunk, hewn square on the sides, was set up

The factory in Sherbrooke, Quebec, in 1899.

and on it the number of enemies killed was represented by painted red figures without heads and prisoners taken by black figures with heads. ... The original post was removed around 1802 and placed in a museum nearby and a new one erected in its place in 1808."[12]

The facility had 3,375 square feet of floor space and 125 employees. A new building was added in 1900, and after the facility was enlarged again in 1906, 400 people worked there. Three years after the formation of the Ingersoll-Rand Company, the North Tarrytown plant was moved to the Painted Post facility, which was enlarged once again.

Right: The first Imperial Type 10 steam-driven compressor built at Painted Post, New York, by the Rand Drill Company. It was shipped December 11, 1900, to the Pullman Company, in Pullman, Illinois. The men were: (from left) C. Rogers, J. Rogers, C. Pitts (shop superintendent), T. Durkin and I. Bronson.

Below: The shop at Sherbrooke in 1902. Pictured from left to right are Al Manning, Hugh Gunning, James Cotter and Will Siler.

is [ultimately the] cheapest, and we will not build or sell any other kind. By building honest, substantial machinery, we do a correspondingly honest and substantial business."[3]

Ingersoll-Sergeant's Rapid Growth

One of the original Ingersoll-Sergeant factories was located at 9th Avenue and 27th Street in New York City. But the company outgrew this facility, moving to Easton, Pennsylvania, in 1894. The vacated New York site was sold in 1905.

"Factory crowding was caused by increased business and the fact that compressors were growing larger and more space was consequently required in which to build them. As expansion of the existing plant was not feasible, a move was the logical solution. Because property was expensive in New York and it was believed that there were advantages in getting away from the city, it was decided to locate outside, although not too far from, the New York headquarters."[4]

Above: To keep pace with increasing demand, Ingersoll-Sergeant sometimes contracted other companies to manufacture equipment, such as this high-pressure compressor, built for Ingersoll-Sergeant by Allis-Chalmers Bullock, Limited, in Montreal.

Easton was chosen partly because of an excellent transportation system, including railroads. The move was directed by George R. Elder,

1894 — Ingersoll-Sergeant begins operations in Easton, Pennsylvania.

1896 — *Compressed Air Magazine* established by W.L. Saunders.

1902 — The Type X portable compressor line is introduced by Rand.

1896 — J. George Leyner invents the hammer drill.

1897 — Rand manufactures Calyx Core drill.

Right: After winning the National League championship in 1904, the New York Giants went on a barnstorming tour during which they visited Easton to play the Ingersoll-Sergeant team. Members of both teams are: seated in front row, Giants Red Ames, Dan McGann, Billy Gilbert, Mike Donlin, and George Browne. Giants in middle row, George Wiltse, Christy Mathewson, Jack Dunn, Bill Dahlen, Sandow Mertes and Al Warner; Ingersoll team standing, George Stillwagon, Jack Stansbury, Frank Mattes, Jim Lavelle, Jack Fuge, J.A.G. Stitzer, Charles Weidenbach, Harry Albus, Billy Flynn, Massey Eckert, Whitey Miller, Charley Walton and Bill Jago.

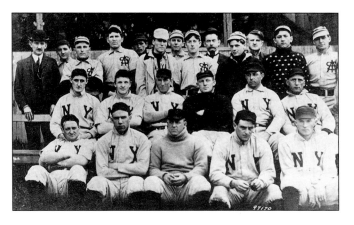

who would become vice president of Ingersoll-Sergeant, and the Easton factory was opened officially on November 1, 1894.

The Easton plant operated 10 hours a day with nearly 200 workers. By this time, more than 10,000 Ingersoll and Sergeant drills had been made, and they were believed to be used in virtually every country around the world. After just one year, the plant was expanded and new equipment was added. But even this expansion was inadequate to handle the flourishing business, and the company elected to open another factory in nearby Phillipsburg, New Jersey. The Phillipsburg factory was built on high ground, avoiding the periodic flooding that plagued the Easton facility. The two plants were relatively close to one another, so it was a simple matter to share both equipment and parts.

"On October 1, 1903, the new foundry turned its first castings — small compressor parts and miniatures of weights used on the rock drill tripod invented by Simon Ingersoll. Meanwhile, frenzied construction of additional capacity continued. The [Phillipsburg] plant's 18 buildings contained 3,000 tons of steel and provided 480,000 square feet of floor space.

1903 — Phillipsburg, New Jersey, plant is established by Ingersoll-Sergeant.

1904 — Branch of Ingersoll-Sergeant established in Paris.

1903 — Imperial Pneumatic Tool Company of Athens, Pennsylvania, joins Rand Drill.

1905 — Patent awarded for Temple-Ingersoll drill.

DAVIS-CALYX DRILL CO.
128 BROADWAY, N.Y.

Dec 1st 1904

I wonder if you would drop me a line? I want to tell you something about those awful Black Diamonds.

Cordially
Cora Calyx

Something of a landmark was the 202-foot-high brick chimney serving the powerhouse."[5]

By 1904, the factory at Phillipsburg was completed and functional, employing more than 1,000 people.

There was a distinct feeling of optimism and camaraderie at Ingersoll-Sergeant. Workers played on the company's football and baseball teams, and in 1904, the Ingersoll-Sergeant team played baseball with National Pennant winners, the New York Giants.

In 1903, W.R. Grace was president of Ingersoll-Sergeant and George Doubleday was treasurer. William Prellwitz, who had been factory chief engineer since 1900, remained chief engineer until his death in 1932.[6]

Innovations from Rand

While Ingersoll-Sergeant continued to grow, the Rand Drill Company was also experiencing success, though at a slightly slower pace. The Calyx Core drill, invented by Francis Harley Davis, was one of the first drill designs produced by Rand. Davis, an Australian, received a patent for it in Victoria in 1893, and another in Western Australia in 1894. The Calyx Core drill was less expensive than drills with the diamond drill bits that were often used for core drilling. Rising diamond costs prompted the innovation, as Vivian explained.

"There was thus created a demand for less expensive core-drilling equipment. It was met by modifying the Davis drill to use crushed steel shot under the cutting edges of a hollow cylindrical bit. The original toothed bit was all right in earth or the softest rocks, but of no value in the harder ones where the diamond drill was being used. Someone had discovered that steel shot became very hard when dropped into cold water while molten, and that crushing it produced angular fragments that would cut most rocks readily."[7]

Left: Cora Calyx, an imaginary correspondent created by Philip Kobbe to publicize the Calyx drill. The black diamonds mentioned in her letter were used in competitive drills, but the Calyx drill gained popularity by using crushed steel shot instead of the increasingly expensive diamonds.

When Davis arrived in the United States in 1896, he convinced the Rand Drill Company to manufacture the Calyx for evaluation. Apparently the test was successful, for in 1897, directors of the Rand Drill Company voted to form the Davis Calyx Drill Company. The Calyx was used to drill test holes at Niagara Falls in the early 1900s.

Philip Kobbe created the fictional character known as Cora Calyx to advertise the Calyx Core drill in trade magazines. These advertisements attracted considerable attention. In 1902, improvements were made to the Calyx drill. But the Davis Calyx Drill Company was dissolved in 1914.

The Temple-Ingersoll

Ingersoll-Sergeant introduced the Temple-Ingersoll drill, for which Robert Temple received a patent in April 1905. The Temple-Ingersoll used as little as one-third or one-quarter the power of competing drills, and remained popular for nearly two decades.

THE INGERSOLL-SERGEANT DRILL CO.

Manufacturers of

All Types of Air Compressors.

Duplex Compressors, driven by Corliss Engines.

Steam and Belt Driven Compressors for Shop Work.

Water Power Compressors, run by Pelton Wheel or Turbine.

SEND FOR CATALOGUE.

THE INGERSOLL SERGEANT DRILL CO.
Havemeyer Building, New York.

AIR COMPRESSORS,
CHANNELERS,
ROCK DRILLS,
COAL CUTTERS.

"The Temple-Ingersoll drill was operated by pulsations of compressed air created by a pulsator actuated by an electric motor, a direct-current type being preferred. Air was never exhausted, but was used over and over again, playing back and forth in a closed circuit. The drill was a very simple piston type, consisting of a cylinder containing a moving piston and a rotation device, with no valves, chest, buffers, springs, side rods, or pawls."[8]

Above: This advertisement appeared in the May 1896 issue of *Compressed Air Magazine.*

Left: A class G-1 steam-driven air compressor from Ingersoll-Sergeant, circa 1899.

The Ingersoll-Sergeant Drill Company obtained an exclusive license for the Temple electric-air patents in May 1905, only a week before the company merged with Rand.

W.L. Saunders, president of Ingersoll-Sergeant and subsequently Ingersoll-Rand, praised the Temple-Ingersoll drill in a 1907 speech to the American Institute of Mining Engineers, declaring that "the unit solved completely the long-baffling problem of employing electric current for driving a rock drill."[9]

In 1905, Ingersoll-Sergeant introduced the Little Jap hammer drill, a modification of a Haeseler pneumatic hammer. It was available in three sizes. The principal drawback of the Little Jap drill was its name. Crews at mining sites never seemed certain what the salesmen were talking about, unsure if they were actually referring to a drill.

Ingersoll Air Compressors

In addition to drills, both companies sold the air compressors that converted air to power for the drills. Though the first portable compressors were sold at the turn of the century, the concept was envisioned at Rand Drill as early as 1888.

"One of the earliest conceptions of a truly portable air plant was on the drafting board at Rand Drill Company in 1888. There is no record that the machine was built, although it is entire-

Left: An advertisement for the Little Jap hammer drill, manufactured by Ingersoll-Sergeant, appearing on the cover of *Compressed Air Magazine* in 1904.

Right: A Little Jap hammer drill being used to excavate the Central Union Gas Company near Freeman Street and Westchester Avenue in the Bronx, about 1907. The operator's necktie and white shirt suggest that he might be a foreman or salesman pressed into service by the photographer.

An engraving of a Class A compressor, the first compressor in the Ingersoll line. Sales of this straight-line model spanned the decades from the 1880s to the early 1900s.

ly possible that one or several of them were produced on special orders. A blueprint of it, dated April 27, 1888, was found in the Portable Compressor Engineering Department at Painted Post in 1959. The machine combined a straight-line, steam-driven compressor, vertical boiler and air storage tank on a wooden-wheeled truck."[10]

John Hickey, who began working for Ingersoll Rock Drill in 1871, was assigned the task of developing and manufacturing an air compressor. He remained with Ingersoll, Ingersoll-Sergeant and ultimately Ingersoll-Rand for 50 years. Unfortunately, no patent is attributed to him, so it is impossible to give him credit for any specific innovation.

Throughout the 1880s, the Ingersoll line of air compressors consisted of straight-line models,

with a common axis for the cylinders and frame. Later models were of the duplex design, with two parallel sets of compressing elements driven by a common crankshaft. The straight-line Class A air compressor was so popular, it was still being sold 30 years after its introduction. During the 1880s, Class A air compressors were used in construction of the tunnels that are today part of the Pennsylvania Turnpike between Harrisburg and Pittsburgh. The Class A compressor was also used during construction of both the Vosburg tunnel in the Lehigh Valley Railroad, and the Hudson River tunnel approaches to New York City.

Rand Air Compressors

Shortly after the turn of the century, Rand introduced the Imperial Type X, or Type 10, a

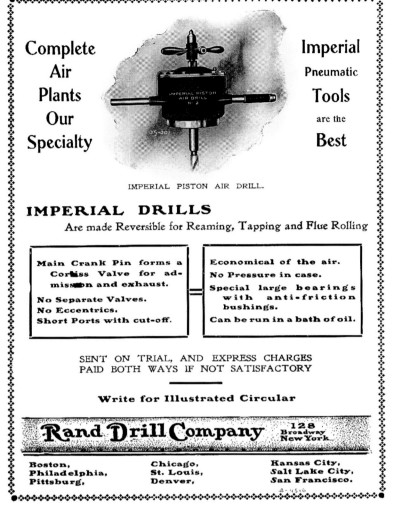

Above: An early advertisement for Imperial pneumatic tools, appearing in *Compressed Air Magazine* in 1903. During this period, Rand Drill was the sales agent for Imperial tools, a company that it would acquire in 1907.

compact, fast-operating unit that gave the greatest capacity per unit of floor space of any compressor at the time. It could be driven directly by steam, or indirectly by belt, gears or silent chain. The recommended operating speeds for both operations was 200 rpm for an 8-inch stroke to 120 rpm for 36-inch sizes. These numbers were conservative, contrary to the claims of competitors who declared the speeds were excessive. The Type X compressor was developed by F.W. Parsons Sr. "Parsons' objective was to standard-

ize a compressor that could be built for stock, which the Rands had never done. He felt that a few sizes ready for immediate delivery would get the bulk of the business."[11]

The Type XI compressor, which originated at Rand, was introduced around 1902, and was successful for more than a decade. It was ultimately phased out as technology advanced, and in 1913 all remaining stock was sold, replaced by the Type XII. Type XIIs were popular for both painting and tire inflation duties. The Eclipse Air Brush Company of Newark was among the many customers of this product.

High-Pressure Compressors

Both Ingersoll-Sergeant and Rand Drill had designs for high-pressure compressors, with various models represented in early literature. Ingersoll-Sergeant began designs for high-pressure compressors in the 1890s, and Rand Drill designs date back nearly as far. High-pressure compressors have been used for a wide variety of jobs, from firing guns to powering locomotives.

"During the Spanish-American War, the U.S. gunboat Vesuvius *was equipped with three compressed air guns, each 55 feet long. They fired projectiles weighing from 400 to 1,000 pounds with air supplied by a mechanical compressor at a maximum pressure of 1,000 pounds per square inch (psi). A shell carrying 500 pounds of explosives could be fired a mile. Similar weapons, capable of being elevated and trained, and called compressed air torpedo guns, were developed for coast defense. Five were manufactured and used experimentally at Sandy Hook, New Jersey, and San Francisco."*[12]

At the beginning of the twentieth century, these compressors were used to power locomotives.

"Probably the greatest single commercial use for high-pressure air for a few years before and after 1900 was for operating compressed air locomotives. ... These haulage units became popular in mines, and especially coal mines, because they emitted no smoke, would not ignite gas, were normally

not seriously damaged by roof falls or derailments and, in case of accident or wreck, provided a source of air for operating tools to help restore conditions."[13]

The Corliss Engine

One air compressor power source used by Ingersoll and Rand was the Corliss steam engine, designed by George Henry Corliss. Along with traditional compressed air applications, compressors driven by Corliss steam engines were widely used to power pumping and hoisting equipment throughout the mining industry. Although initially more expensive, it was more economical in the long run because of increased fuel efficiency, in some cases using less than half the coal required to operate other machines. A 1906 Ingersoll-Rand catalog further explained the popularity of the Corliss.

"The Corliss steam engine is recognized as the most durable and economical type of engine. Its structural solidity, the simplicity of its valve gear and its graceful outlines, combined with the faithfulness with which it blends practice and theory in reducing all engine losses to a minimum, are largely the cause of its present popularity in the engineering world. It is especially well adapted as the power end of a compressor of the highest type, where the production of the working fluid must be low in cost and the parts so designed as to withstand the severe strains of air-compressing work."[14]

When Ingersoll-Rand consolidated its compressor lines, it devoted less attention to the Corliss engine, which declined in popularity and was discontinued in 1930.

By 1905, when the two companies merged, Rand marketed six basic compressor styles, while the Ingersoll-Sergeant line was represented by nine. Though both companies were successful, Ingersoll-Sergeant compressors were considered superior.[15]

Early Labor Unions

Both Ingersoll-Sergeant and Rand Drill had labor unions, and both companies experienced labor strikes in the 1890s. Ingersoll-Sergeant workers in Easton went on strike in January 1896, in a dispute over pay for piecework. Workers argued that their wages were being reduced. W.R. Grace, president of Ingersoll-Sergeant, argued that the lower per-piece earnings would increase productivity. The strike continued for weeks, but produc-

Above: An Ingersoll-Sergeant Class JC compressor, built around 1900 for discharge pressures of 110 to 700 pounds per square inch (psi). Various models weighed from 5,000 to 38,100 pounds. The intercooler was in the base, connecting the low-pressure cylinder on the right with the high-pressure cylinder on the left.

Left: An Ingersoll-Sergeant air compressor, driven by an electric motor, was available by 1899.

WHEN GOLD was discovered in Western Australia in the late nineteenth century, both Ingersoll-Sergeant and the Rand Drill Company played a key role in mining the precious metal. By 1890, both companies had representatives serving a thriving market.

An Ingersoll-Rand subsidiary was incorporated in 1923, and Ingersoll-Rand's first Australian factory was established in South Melborne in 1935. A plant opened in 1970 in Dandenong produces a wide range of products, including stationary air compressors, pumps for process industries and

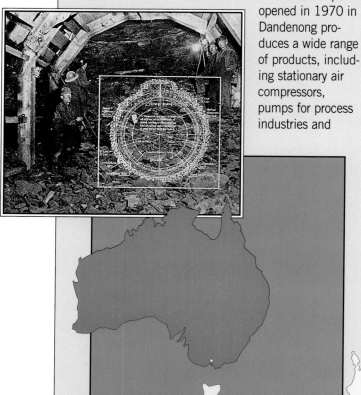

Australia

power plants, and soil and asphalt compactors for construction. Torrington also is located in Dandenong. Subsidiaries in Australia include Ingersoll-Rand (Australia) Limited and Ingersoll-Dresser Pumps (Australia) Private Limited. One Ingersoll-Rand plant is in neighboring Auckland, New Zealand.

tion continued because replacement workers had been hired.[16]

To appease workers, Grace made charitable donations to the Catholic church and to other groups. During the strike, the union gave its members $6 a week if they were married and $4 if they were single, but it did not provide legal support for members or get involved in negotiation. Eventually, the strike lost momentum. Some workers returned to the plant, while other chose not to return.[17]

The Rand organization experienced some labor disputes in its Tarrytown, New York, plant during this same time period, but few details have survived.

Competition

During the 1890s, both Rand Drill and Ingersoll-Sergeant manufactured virtually identical equipment for mining. Both companies were expanding into England, Australia, and other countries where mining equipment was needed. As the territories of the two companies began to overlap, rivalry increased, noted Vivian. "As Ingersoll spread out into the mining field and Rand entered into contracting and general construction, competition between the two companies steadily increased, and this rivalry was reflected in the sales literature [and advertising] of both concerns."[18]

The first advertisement for an Ingersoll drill was in January 1874. Under the headline, "Ingersoll's Improved Rock Drill for Use in Mines, Tunnels, Shafts, Gadding," the text emphasized the exclusive automatic feed feature. Competitors such as Burleigh, Rand & Waring, Diamond, Gardiner and Wood were mentioned by name, and the advertisement featured a picture of a tripod-mounted drill.

A few months later, another advertisement featured a drawing of two caricatures clinging to the top and bottom of a world globe, using a tripod-mounted drill. This symbolized the worldwide use of the drill, and was later adopted as the trademark of the Ingersoll Rock Drill Company.[19]

Comparative figures often were given in advertisements to compare the actual feet drilled by different kinds of drills. Not surprisingly, the statistics always seemed to support the company doing the advertising. Of 10 advertisements from different drill companies on a single page of the April 17, 1875 edition of *The Engineering and Mining Journal*, two had competitive figures — the Rand & Waring Drill and Compressor Company, and the Ingersoll Rock Drill Company.

The advertisement from Rand & Waring listed the amount of feet drilled by three types of drills at the Port Henry Mine. According to the ad, Rand drilled a total of 918 feet, Ingersoll drilled 545 feet, and Waring drilled 136 feet. However, on the same page, the advertisement from the Ingersoll Rock Drill Company suggested a different result. Their ad pointed out that Ingersoll had drilled 545 feet with one drill, while Rand had required three drills for 918 feet.

Trade publications, such as *The Engineering and Mining Journal*, demonstrate that competition was keen before the turn of the century. Competitors included the Sullivan Machinery Company, McKiernan Rock Drill Company, Denver Rock Drill Company, and The American Diamond Drill Company.

"The two pioneer concerns, Ingersoll-Sergeant and Rand, were doing the bulk of the business in their lines. Both had resourceful engineering staffs and capable executive direction that enabled them to take advantage of the wonderful opportunities that were afforded them. Both registered healthy growth and became vigorous and prosperous. As time went on, there was less tendency for Rand to concentrate on mining and Ingersoll on tunnel-

Advertisements from the April 17, 1875, issue of *The Engineering and Mining Journal* reveal early competition between the Ingersoll Rock Drill Company and the Rand & Waring Drill and Compressor Company.

ing and contracting. Each began to enter all fields of possible business."[20]

Despite this competition, Vivian noted, the two companies were "always on 'speaking terms,' and this made it possible for them to get together, after some preliminary sparring, when the time became ripe for their merger."[21]

A Class E electric-driven compressor, built for a construction company in 1906.

A Gordon-Ingersoll hammer drill being tested in a traditional granite block at Phillipsburg, New Jersey, in 1907.

CHAPTER FOUR

INGERSOLL-RAND

"I must be satisfied that I could not only accept for myself and my friends the stocks in a new company in exchange for our shares, but that I should be so convinced of its advisability as to enable me to strongly recommend the shareholders to accept such exchange."

— Michael P. Grace's criteria
for approving Ingersoll-Rand merger

B Y 1905, BOTH Ingersoll and Rand held important patents that advanced the technology of drills and compressors, and both were leaders in the industry. It has been lost to history which company approached the other and suggested a union. Details of an agreement were discussed at an Ingersoll-Sergeant meeting held in London, some of which was documented in *The Mining World and Engineering Record* of July 22, 1905.

When William Russell Grace died in 1904, William L. Saunders became president of Ingersoll-Sergeant. Grace's younger brother, Michael P. Grace, became a guiding force in the company. In reporting to stockholders at an Ingersoll-Sergeant meeting in July 1905, Michael Grace voiced concern over the proposed merger.

"I consented, for the first time, to consider the matter; but on these conditions, which I put to [Ingersoll-Sergeant President William Saunders] with absolute clearness: (1) I would not advise any combination which deprived the company of the able management which had made it a signal success in the past. (2) I would not advise any combination on the basis of inflated capital. In plain English, any company formed must have for every dollar of bonds or stock issued repre- *sented by actual liquid assets, real estate, buildings, machinery and inventory — absolutely excluding goodwill and patents rights. Not that goodwill and patents are not valuable; they are very valuable, but they must be treated as reserve and not be considered as capital. (3) The third condition was that I must, after personal examination on the spot, be satisfied that I could not only accept for myself and my friends the stocks in a new company in exchange for our shares, but that I should be so convinced of its advisability as to enable me to strongly recommend the shareholders to accept such exchange."*[1]

Grace's inspection apparently met his criteria, and ultimately the merger was approved. At the time of the merger, the total value of Ingersoll-Sergeant shares was $7,145,157.11 and the total value of Rand Drill was $2,346,548.88. To adjust for their respective values, Ingersoll-Sergeant retained 75.3 percent of the new stock issued and Rand retained 24.7 percent.[2] The new Ingersoll-Rand Company was incorporated June 1, 1905,

Above: A Rogler plate valve for a compressor from 1913.

Left: Michael P. Grace, brother of W.R. Grace, was chairman of Ingersoll-Sergeant for a time, and played an important role in the 1905 merger.

but the merger did not formally take effect until December 27, 1905, when stockholders of both companies met separately and voted to "accept the offers made to them by Ingersoll-Rand to acquire their assets."[3]

Ingersoll-Sergeant President W.L. Saunders became president of the newly formed Ingersoll-Rand. George Doubleday, former treasurer of Ingersoll-Sergeant, became vice president. Jasper R. Rand, former president of Rand Drill, also became vice president, as did John A. McCall, J. Peter Grace and George R. Elder. W.R. Grace was treasurer, and Fred A. Brainerd was secretary.

Working out the Details

The main office for Ingersoll-Rand was at 11 Broadway, the Bowling Green building, a historic New York City address. Even in 1905, the office was easy to reach by train. The headquarters remained at this location until 1972, when a new headquarters was built in suburban Woodcliff Lake, New Jersey.

The merger of Ingersoll-Sergeant and Rand Drill was a popular issue with the press. The media was preoccupied that Ingersoll-Rand might be so huge that no other company could compete, leading to fears that Ingersoll-Rand would set

1904 — William L. Saunders becomes president of Ingersoll-Sergeant.

1905 — The Ingersoll-Sergeant Drill Company merges with the Rand Drill Company.

1904 — Ingersoll-Rand compressors and drills are put to work on the Panama Canal.

The warehouse for Ingersoll-Rand at 20 Washington Street in New York City. The company still has offices in all the principal cities of the world.

1907 — Imperial Pneumatic Tool Company is acquired.

1910 — The Class OC 4-stage compressor is introduced.

1909 — Ingersoll-Rand acquires A.S. Cameron Steam Pump Works of New York City.

1906 — Class J motor-driven compressor is introduced.

Right: The Class NE-1 12-inch-stroke compressor with a piston valve inlet. The Class NE was an improved version of the E and was improved continually over the years.

means of a screw. When the receiver pressure rose above normal, the pressure was communicated through a small pipe to a piston that closed the valve against spring pressure."[17]

In 1907, two new duplex compressors were introduced, the Class O, which was steam-driven, and the Class P, which was belt-driven. The Class O design became the Class OC in 1910, one of two new Corliss steam-powered models introduced during that period. The other was called the Class CH. The OC model was faster than previous Corliss machines, and was manufactured in 40 sizes. This model evolved into the ORC

when Rogler valves were added, and into the ORD when a poppet type of steam valve was incorporated. The ORD enjoyed success for more than a decade, but by 1933 the market for steam-driven compressors had virtually disappeared.

The pneumatic tool business was also important to the new company. The two Ingersoll-Rand

This Class NE-1 compressor, driven by electric motor, was built in 1913 for the Warner Gear Company of New York.

predecessors had decided independently to affiliate with established pneumatic tool businesses rather than start from scratch with their own lines. Rand was an exclusive sales agent for the Imperial Pneumatic Tool Company of Athens, Pennsylvania, and Ingersoll-Sergeant had acquired control of the Haeseler Pneumatic Tool Company of Philadelphia. When Ingersoll and Rand merged, Ingersoll-Rand acquired the assets of the Haeseler-Ingersoll Pneumatic Tool Company. The Imperial Pneumatic Tool Company became part of the company in 1907.

Right: A Haeseler-Ingersoll wood-boring drill, used here to lay tracks for the Williamsburg Bridge connecting Manhattan and Brooklyn. The suspension bridge, completed in 1904, had two tracks for elevated railway cars and two for surface electric cars. Materials included 650 tons of 80-pound rails, 1 million feet of lumber, and 150 tons of bolts and washers.

Below: A partly dismantled main bearing of a Class OC compressor. Introduced in 1910, the duplex Class OC was an advance over Class O of 1907 and featured massive bearings.

Railroads, shipyards, foundries and stone-working establishments were the principal early customers of pneumatic tools, with railroads easily the most important of these and shipyards second in importance.

Cameron Pumps

In 1909, Ingersoll-Rand paid $1 million to acquire A.S. Cameron Steam Pump Works, a business founded in 1860 in New York by Adam Scott Cameron. Since Cameron's death in 1877, the company had been run by his widow, Julia E. Cameron. Though Cameron became a division of Ingersoll-Rand, its pumps continued to carry the Cameron name through 1964. The pump indus-

Cameron vertical feed pump, in the boiler room of the *USS North Carolina,* in 1909, the year Ingersoll-Rand acquired Cameron assets. The entire pump equipment on the cruiser consisted of 27 Cameron pumps.

try was a strategic diversification for Ingersoll-Rand, because pumps are vital to a wide variety of industry, as historian C.H. Vivian pointed out.

"One can hardly think of an industry that doesn't use pumps, and our daily lives are importantly affected by them. The water and milk we drink, the gasoline we burn in our cars are pumped one or more times before they reach us; our clothing, newspapers, the brick, steel and lumber that go into our homes and buildings and the

Left: This combined pump and boiler was pictured in the Cameron catalog of 1900. The unit needed only connection to a suction and discharge pipe to be ready to work.

electricity that lights the structures, all require the service of pumps in their making. It has been authoritatively reported that the number of pumps produced each year exceeds the total of all automobiles, refrigerators and electric motors."[18]

As Cameron's New York factory became too small to handle the increasing production of pumps, a new factory, roughly three times as large, was built in Phillipsburg, New Jersey, adjacent to Ingersoll-Rand's facility.

Advertising

Before the merger, C.B. Morse headed the advertising department for Ingersoll-Sergeant,

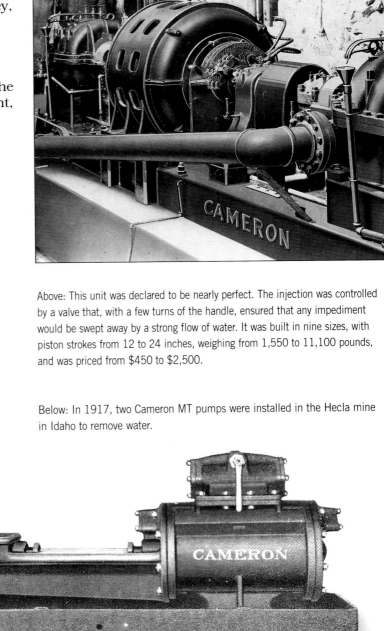

Above: This unit was declared to be nearly perfect. The injection was controlled by a valve that, with a few turns of the handle, ensured that any impediment would be swept away by a strong flow of water. It was built in nine sizes, with piston strokes from 12 to 24 inches, weighing from 1,550 to 11,100 pounds, and was priced from $450 to $2,500.

Below: In 1917, two Cameron MT pumps were installed in the Hecla mine in Idaho to remove water.

and Philip Kobbe was in charge of advertising for Rand Drill. After the merger, separate advertising departments were maintained for about six months, at which time Kobbe retired, and the advertising departments were combined, with Lucius Wightman in charge. He had the unusual task of promoting equipment that had been his competition only a year earlier.

In the early 1960s, C.H. Vivian made note of the conservative nature of Ingersoll-Rand's advertising practices.

"Ingersoll-Rand has always conducted an adequate and sound advertising and publicity program. Expressed

as a percentage of gross sales income, annual expenditures for this purpose have been comparatively modest. Except for occasional and minor departures in the case of pneumatic tools and merchandising products, advertising copy and layouts have traditionally been conservative and dignified."[19]

Compressed Air Magazine, started by William Saunders in 1896, now boasts a circulation of 130,000. Published by Ingersoll-Rand, it reports on the management of technology in the fields of transportation, construction, manufacturing, and the petrochemical industry.

In 1906, the company began direct-mail advertising, making it among the first companies in the United States to use this approach. Direct mailings were more expensive than generic advertisements, but the technique was effective. Lists of customers and prospective customers were compiled and organized, and by 1912, a list of 200,000 names was available.

"The first letter was mailed to railroads and was followed by a series of eight mailings to manufactured gas distributors. Their industry was not being reached effectively by trade journal advertisements and, as a number of compressor orders had been received, especially in the Chicago territory, it was considered worthwhile to conduct the mail campaign. The cost of preparing and mailing the eight letters was more than $1,000, which was considered a large expenditure for such a purpose in those days." [20]

Another marketing tool was *Compressed Air Magazine*, the magazine first begun by Saunders in 1896 at Ingersoll-Sergeant. Saunders continued to oversee the magazine until his retirement in 1931. Vivian, the magazine's editor from 1932 to 1957, described the magazine in 1966.

"Compressed Air Magazine is believed to be the oldest American publication of its kind — a trade paper that solicits outside advertising and is put out by an industrial manufacturing firm. In fact, there are few other publications in its category. ... The aim is to present interesting and mostly nontechnical accounts of operations in which the company's equipment is used." [21]

The first issue of *Compressed Air* contained 16 pages. In the 1920s, the cover was predominantly red. When it was suggested that this color should change from month to month, W.R. Grace himself said he would prefer that it remained red for easy identification. Although the cover is never entirely red today, an identifiable red square remains on the cover to continue the long tradition. The original subscription price was $1 a year, and by 1913 there were 15,000 subscribers. In 1994, the magazine consisted of 52 pages, published in full color and with a phenomenal pass-along audience of 635,000 readers.

Before the merger, Rand also had a publication, called *Air Power*, intended to compete

AIR TOOLS

"HAESELER" AND "IMPERIAL"

Two distinct lines of established superiority. Marked by novel and correct design, selected materials specially treated, unsurpassed workmanship, and absolute interchangeability of parts. Simple, economical, low in repair charges, reliable under every condition. Built for hard and effective service, in shops, foundries, shipyards, and structural works.

CHIPPING AND RIVETING HAMMERS, ROTARY AND RECIPROCATING DRILLS, HOISTS, RIVETERS, REAMERS, ETC.

The illustrations show a Haesler hammer at work on the casson structure of the Paris Subway, France; and an Imperial Wood Boring Machine at work in a shipyard.

INGERSOLL RAND CO.

11 Broadway, NEW YORK.

Cleveland, O.	St. Louis, Mo.
Philadelphia, Pa.	Chicago, Ill.
Pittsburg, Pa.	Houghton, Mich.
El Paso, Tex.	Boston, Mass.

Above: This advertisement from *Compressed Air Magazine* in 1906 is for both the Haeseler and Imperial tool lines offered by the newly formed Ingersoll-Rand Company. Notice in the advertisement that the company name is not hyphenated as it always is found now.

with *Compressed Air Magazine*. Only four issues were published, between January and October of 1905. When the companies merged, *Air Power* was discontinued.

The ability of Jackhamer drills to drill at any angle was important in shaping the Mount Rushmore memorial in South Dakota (see page 75).

CHAPTER FIVE

THE DOUBLEDAY YEARS

"Long after retirement at age 65 had become the general rule, the leading company in the U.S. industry was run by a man of 89. The company was Ingersoll-Rand Company, unquestionably the most successful machinery maker in the United States. The man was George Doubleday."

— Forbes, 1965.

ON APRIL 30, 1913, William L. Saunders was elected Ingersoll-Rand's first chairman of the board, a position he would hold until 1931. This left vacant the position of president. George Doubleday, who had been hired away from the Terminal Warehouse Company by William Russell Grace in 1894, became Ingersoll-Rand's second president. W.R.'s grandson, J. Peter Grace, explained how Doubleday joined the company.

"One day, a young, 15-year-old messenger from the warehouse brought a packet of documents for my grandfather to sign. Grandfather was immediately impressed by the young lad, and observed him closely for the few minutes they were together. He then asked the messenger to wait outside, and my grandfather phoned the president of the warehouse company. He asked the president for permission to hire the young messenger. Feeling unable to refuse the modest request of his largest client, the warehouse president agreed. The young man, George Doubleday, was hired on the spot."[1]

Doubleday started as an auditor and rose through the ranks of Ingersoll-Sergeant and then Ingersoll-Rand.

When Ingersoll-Rand was formed, Doubleday became first vice president of the new company. He became president of Ingersoll-Rand in 1913. In 1936, Doubleday became chairman of the board, a post he held until 1955.

"Doubleday devoted practically all his life to building the company. He was known for his financial acumen and was a keen judge of men and their fitness for doing the jobs he assigned them. He was the opposite of Saunders in one respect. He shunned publicity, made no public appearances and gave no interviews."[2]

A 1965 *Forbes* article commented on Doubleday's remarkable durability. "Long after retirement at age 65 had become the general rule, the leading company in the U.S. industry was run by a man of 89. The company was Ingersoll-Rand Company, unquestionably the most successful machinery maker in the United States. The man was George Doubleday."[3]

Above: An oil-burning furnace developed by J. George Leyner in 1912, used for heating drill steel prior to forging the ends.

George Doubleday (seated right), who seldom posed for the camera, had the longest service record of any member of Ingersoll-Rand.

Doubleday had a keen memory for people he had met, as this incident recalled by retired salesman Walter Leutwyler indicates.

"I was working for Sulzer Bros. of Switzerland as a young engineer, and they sent me on the shake-down voyage of a cruise ship as part of the sales and installation contract on the big main propulsion diesel engines they had furnished. It was there that I got acquainted with Mr. George Doubleday, then president of Ingersoll-Rand, who was returning from a tour of Ingersoll-Rand's British and European facilities. At the conclusion of the voyage, Mr. Doubleday said that Ingersoll-Rand made diesel engines, and if I ever thought of leaving my native Switzerland, I should come and see him in New York City.

1912 — Ingersoll-Rand acquires J.G. Leyner Engineering Works Company.

1913 — W.L. Saunders becomes the company's first chairman and George Doubleday becomes president.

1920 — Type 20 portable compressor is introduced.

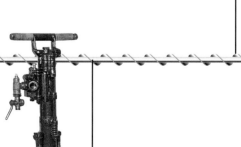

1912 — Jackhamer drill is invented.

1915 — During World War I, Ingersoll-Rand produced shell casings in addition to its air compressors and drills.

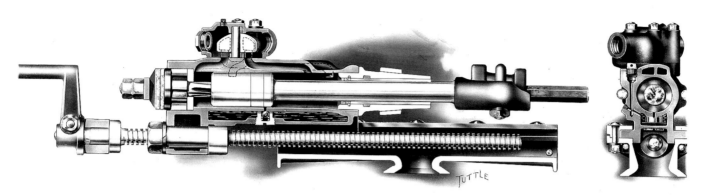

A sketch of an Ingersoll-Rand Model C-110 Butterfly valve rock drill from 1913. The Butterfly valve permitted faster operation than before.

"I thought nothing of it until a year or so later, when I fell in love, got married, and needed a job in the United States. Unfortunately, I had not written down Mr. Doubleday's name or address. I remembered him only as 'Mr. Ingersoll-Rand.' I looked him up in the phone book in New York and there he was, at 11 Broadway! I went to the 14th floor, and a man in a dark suit behind a counter asked me who I had an appointment with. I said, 'Mr. Ingersoll Rand.' He was trying to tell me that there was no Mr. Ingersoll-Rand, when by pure chance, Mr. Doubleday came *walking down the corridor and recognized me! He took me into his office and I got hired."*[4]

Despite his modest demeanor, Doubleday was an aggressive businessman. From the time he became first vice president to the time he retired from the chairmanship, sales increased from $7 million to $130 million annually, earnings from $1.27 million to $23 million, and the number of employees from 300 to 8,000.[5] This growth was achieved through a combination of acquisition and new product development.

1922 — Ingersoll-Rand South Africa Incorporated.

1927 — Ingersoll-Rand provides Jackhamer drills for work on Mount Rushmore.

1921 — Ingersoll-Rand (India) Private Ltd. formed.

1925 — First diesel-electric locomotive sold to Central Railroad of New Jersey.

1929 — Pneumatic angle wrench is designed.

Leyner's Contributions

John George Leyner was born in a Colorado mining community in 1860, and his first few jobs were with mining and milling companies. In 1891, established as J. George Leyner, Machinist, he began designing hammer drills, which were easier to use and more economical than piston drills.

Hammer drills tended to break down after hard use. Since spare parts were difficult to find, contractors returned to using Ingersoll-Rand piston drills, which were easier to repair. Ingersoll-Rand had been trying to create competing drills that would not infringe on Leyner's patents. By 1911, the company settled on the strategy of purchasing Leyner's company. It paid $30 each for 3,039 shares of Leyner's common stock, gaining voting control of the company and a license to use Leyner's drills by paying a royalty.

In 1912, Leyner became an employee of Ingersoll-Rand, earning $5,600 a year and retaining rights to his 39 patents, which included 22 for rock drills, and six for compressors.[6] Leyner continued to invent, but his career was tragically ended by an automobile accident in 1920.

"Authorities agree that J. George Leyner, by changing the principle of mechanical drilling, contributed more to modern rock drill design than any other individual. Almost all modern drills utilize the basic features that Leyner introduced, modified and improved over time. Leyner's great accomplishment was of course, to change the action of the mechanical drill from one of plunging or punching, to that of hammering."[7]

After the acquisition of Leyner's company, Ingersoll-Rand engineers were able to use Leyner's patented features in their new designs. Leyner's patents went toward developing the stoping drill, used for mining ore from steeply inclined or vertical veins. Stopers drill vertical holes, while drifters are for horizontal holes. *Compressed Air Magazine* attributes the invention of the hammer-type stoping drill to C.H. Shaw in the late 1880s. C.H. Vivian noted, however, that Shaw's name does not appear in patent

A Bull Moose hammer drill, invented by A.H. Taylor in Easton in 1909.

records until 1905. With the help of Leyner, the trademark name, Stopehamer, was registered in 1916. The Jackstoper, introduced in 1929, was used for wet drilling.

The Jackhamer

The Jackhamer, introduced in 1912, was Leyner's most enduring success. A hand-held drill with automatic rotation, the Jackhamer was easier to handle, more reliable, and easier to repair than previous hammer drills. It featured a hollow steel drill through which air and water could be directed to clear the hole of cuttings.

"The development of the Jackhamer was a high point in the evolution of drilling equipment

The first wagon drill to be shipped to a customer went to work in 1925 in the quarry of J.L. Shiely Company, St. Paul, Minnesota.

and had far-reaching effects. It revolutionized downhole drilling practice and eased the lot of the underground worker in most types of mining. It likewise helped sound the doom of the heavy tripod mounting in ordinary drilling practice."[8]

By 1921, the Jackhamer was manufactured in five different sizes and used for road building, foundation work, and any general downhole work. The name *Jackhamer* was so widely used that it came to refer to that type of drill, regardless of the company that manufactured it. One *m* from Jackhammer was dropped so that the name Jackhamer could become a registered trademark.

Though many drills today are referred to as Jackhamers, only Ingersoll-Rand holds the patent for the real thing. "*The New York Times* calls a pavement breaker a Jackhamer half the time," said King Cunningham, who recently retired as vice president of international marketing.[9] Retired Vice President of Sales Bill Austin noted that "a pavement breaker is just an air-operated crow bar. Just a piston. It doesn't drill. It just strikes. And a Jackhamer rotates and has a bit on it and drills a hole."[10]

Drifter Drills

By 1913, Ingersoll-Rand manufactured six different kinds of drills, including the Jackhamer, each with recommended applications as outlined in the company catalog. Drifter drills, which were almost always used in a mounted configuration, were designed for horizontal drilling, mostly in mines and tunnels. These drills were so popular from 1912 through 1914 that production could not keep up with demand and no need was felt to advertise. When Ingersoll-Rand finally advertised drifter drills in 1914, the ads simply gave notice that Ingersoll-Rand was prepared to accept orders for the drills. Manufacturing facilities were continuously expanded to handle the huge demand for the product, which evolved and improved over the years. The Leyner-Ingersoll R-72 drill, designed for tunneling and drifting, was used in some important tunnels in the twenties, including the 6.2-mile Moffat Railroad bore in Colorado, the first long tunnel to penetrate the Continental Divide.[11]

In the thirties and forties, the S-70 model was used on the Colorado River Aqueduct in Southern California, portions of the Delaware Aqueduct, and on the Carlton Tunnel in the Colorado Rockies.

Retouched 1936 photograph of one of the first Type FM wagon drills, an N-75 drifter, mounted on pneumatic tires.

Improved Air Compressors

Continuing research brought about the steady refinement of air compressors during the first half of the twentieth century. The Imperial line of compressors, used in the oil and railroad industries, among other applications, was expanded.

In 1915, the Type XPV steam-driven compressor was introduced.

"The need for a steam-driven machine that could operate satisfactorily, not only under ordinary steam conditions but also with high pressure and superheated steam, became apparent to Ingersoll-Rand prior to 1915 through analyzing sales of compressors abroad. European customers preferred steam-driven compressors that were built there."[15]

The Type XPV was offered in sizes varying from 608 to 3,620 cubic feet per minute (cfm) capacity. Though it had many of the same features that had been successful on the Imperial Type 10, it was designed from scratch as a new steam-driven compressor. Competitors had difficulty copying the unique model. The Ingersoll-Rand XPV set the standard for steam-driven duplex compressors throughout the industry, and was used for many decades.

The Class ER, introduced in 1914, and the FR, introduced a year later, featured Rogler plate valves and were capable of nearly repair-free operation.

"The ER and FR design met the demand for a simple, readily accessible, relatively trouble-

Above, left: The first Type XG compressor, built at Painted Post in 1925. The XG consisted of a two-cylinder, four-cycle gas engine connected to compressor cylinders having full plate valves on both inlet and discharge. The machine enjoyed widespread use in oil fields, but was also employed in industrial service wherever natural or manufactured gas was available.

Left: Two Type XPV compressors ready to be pressed into service at the site of oil well tests in California in the early 1930s.

Tie Tampers

KEEPING RAILROAD tracks in good condition is an expensive and time-consuming task, requiring a large labor force. One of the most difficult parts of the project is tamping ballast under railroad ties. In 1913, Ingersoll-Rand introduced a pneumatic tie tamper that made the job much easier.

The tamper was patented by George W. Vaughn, an employee for the New York Central Railroad, who turned the manufacture of the device over to Ingersoll-Rand.[16]

The tie tamper, which weighed 37½ pounds with a bar in place, was light enough to be handled easily by a railroad worker. The bar had a slight curve at its lower end that allowed it to fit under the entire length of the tie, even where the rails ran. This was impossible with previously conceived tamping appliances. Ingersoll-Rand also introduced a portable air compressor, designed for use with the tie tamper.

The tie tamper and accompanying air compressor helped maintain the network of railroads that were criss-crossing the nation. As the nation industrialized, railroad laborers were increasingly difficult to find, because industrial plants offered higher wages and easier work. Tie tampers helped solve this labor shortage problem, since the work could be done with fewer men, noted historian C.H. Vivian. "At the Chicago terminal of the New York Central Lines, five men and two tampers did the work formerly done by 19 hand-tampers. At a daily wage of $1.90, the saving in the labor of ten men was $19."[17]

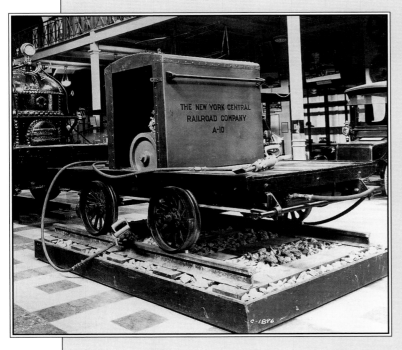

Above, left: An M-1 tie tamper from 1916.

Above: A motor-driven tie tamper compressor from 1917, used for work on electric railroads.

Left: The world's first tie tamper compressor, displayed at the Smithsonian Institution in Washington, D.C., along with two 1914 tie tampers. At the request of Ingersoll-Rand, the New York Central Railroad rehabilitated the compressor for display at the museum. Due to lack of space, the museum returned the machine to New York Central in 1942.

free, reasonably priced unit with good capacity in relation to the floor space occupied. For the first time, it provided small compressors that had many desirable features of larger ones. There was a place for such a machine in a large percentage of the industrial plants."[18]

The Class ES, which replaced the ER in 1933, featured stainless steel channel valves,

lower air speeds, less pressure loss, and lower air temperatures.

World War I

The uneasy peace in Europe was shattered in 1914. Her nations had begun to assemble and deploy modern weapons of war, including airplanes, tanks and submarines. In 1915, Ingersoll-Rand added auxiliary shell casings to its production lines.

The Type XPV, introduced in 1915, set an industry standard for steam-driven duplex compressors. Above are six Type XPV compressors from 1934.

"A newspaper report published January 16, 1915, announced the impending switch in production from rock drills and compressors to munitions as follows:

'The orders at Phillipsburg and Easton are to fill up all departments at once to the limit of 2800 men, whereas two days a week had been the order there for weeks; while scarcely more than 100 men have found employment for some time at Painted Post.'

"Shell making was known among the personnel as the Shell Game. Around 21 or 22 separate operations were required, starting with the piercing, which was done in the Heat Treating Department, with Fred Martin in charge. Many of the individual operations were performed on a piecework basis. Bonuses for exceeding set quotas boosted production, which was sorely needed."[19]

The Phillipsburg plant, as well as the Canadian factory at Sherbrooke, devoted a major portion of its production to turning out artillery shell casings.

Ingersoll-Rand's portable compressors were also critical in the war effort, as Vivian recorded.

A Type XB-$\frac{1}{2}$ vacuum pump, used in the Amity Gasoline Company in Bartlesville, Oklahoma, in 1924.

A Type 10 vacuum pump built at Painted Post in 1917, with a duplex construction to handle varying capacities.

"Ingersoll-Rand portable compressors are probably as universally used as any other piece of American-built machinery, not even excluding automobiles. They serve in war and in peace. During World War I an Austrian general, whose troops were fighting the Italian forces along their common border in the high reaches of the Alps, sent the following telegram to Vienna: 'Send more pneumatic rock drills and compressors. More important than artillery.'"[20]

Even before the war ended, the company was overwhelmed with orders for compressors.

"During the period of lagging business in the early stages of the war, the company had sold some surplus machine tools and had to buy some of them back later when business picked up. This happened near the end of the conflict, when heavy orders for compressors started coming in from abroad because most

A Type XB-1 vacuum pump at work in a Cuban sugar cane processing plant in 1930. Use of Ingersoll-Rand vacuum pumps in Cuban sugar mills began in 1915. This unit had Texrope drive that was patented by Allis-Chalmers.

manufacturers over there were turning out little except war material."[21]

A sense of relief and a return to routine
after the war brought many Ingersoll-Rand
employees together to engage in various recre-
ational activities. Trapshooting was a popular
form of recreation at Phillipsburg after World
War I, and social gatherings were often held at
the Hillcrest Club.

This Class FR-1 Ingersoll-Rand steam-driven vacuum pump, introduced in 1917, featured Rogler valves and was available in five sizes.

Refrigeration

The technology surrounding high-pressure
compressors led to the development of refrigeration compressors, an important new field for
Ingersoll-Rand. With attention focused on valves
and design, faster running compressors suitable
for refrigeration needs were developed.

*"Ice-making appealed to Ingersoll-Rand
because it presented an opportunity to sell
equipment in addition to ammonia compressors: Cameron pumps, for circulating condenser water and brine; compressors to supply 30 pounds per square inch of air during
its freezing; and in some instances air for pro-*

*ducing water from wells by air lift; con-
densers and vacuum pumps in steam-operat-
ed plants; and air hoists for lifting the ice
cans from brine tanks."[22]*

Research and development on the process
of refrigeration also led to the development of
cooling systems first used in trains and buses. A
salesman in India suggested that Ingersoll-Rand
enter the air conditioning business, recalled
King Cunningham, retired vice president of
international marketing.

*"Back in the thirties, Bill Ford wrote to say,
'You know, throughout India, there's a great
potential for air conditioning.' It was taken up
before the board, and the board decided it had
no future. Ford wrote back the next month and
said, 'I'm convinced the world is going to go*

Diesel Locomotives

INGERSOLL-RAND'S work on air compressors led to the creation of an internal combustion engine that revolutionized train travel. The new design worked by using the heat of highly compressed air to ignite a spray of fuel that was introduced after the compression stroke started.

Diesel engines had been patented by German engineer Rudolf Diesel in 1892, but Ingersoll-Rand was the first to create a commercially successful locomotive engine. This innovation prompted the great railroads of the nation to turn away from steam engines and convert to diesels.

By 1920, Ingersoll-Rand was an established diesel engine builder. The company formed a working agreement with General Electric to create a diesel-powered locomotive featuring controls, gear and assembly by General Electric and a truck frame by American Locomotive. Testing began in 1923, and in October 1925, a 300-horsepower unit was sold to the Central Railroad of New Jersey. Known as No. 1000, the durable engine operated for the Central Railroad until 1957.

Because of its historical significance, No. 1000 is now on display at the Baltimore & Ohio's Transportation Museum in Baltimore.

"The oil-electric locomotive operated at a fuel cost about one-fourth that of its steam counterpart. At the time of its introduction it was expected to save $55 million worth of fuel annually for American railroads, even if it were applied solely to switching service. The brilliant future that was forecast for diesel traction has been more than fulfilled, but the fates decreed that Ingersoll-Rand was not to share the profits. Having laid the groundwork for what can be looked back upon as one of the greatest forward strides in the field of transportation, the company withdrew in 1937, and turned its efforts to promoting the 10 x 12-inch diesel for industrial service.

"Many reasons contributed to this decision. First, Ingersoll-Rand was the only member of the manufacturing alliance that was deeply concerned with selling the diesel-electric locomotive. American Locomotive Company built steam units and General Electric built electric units and it was natural that they should push them in preference to a product in which they had only a part interest. This left it up to Ingersoll-Rand to shoulder the major burden of the selling effort. In time this became onerous."[23]

Railroad representatives from around the United States gathered to witness the testing of a new 100-ton oil-electric locomotive for the Long Island Railroad in 1925.

Above: This is how the coming of the oil-electric locomotive was depicted in 1927 by Winsor McCay, a leading New York newspaper cartoonist. The absence of smoke for its operation in cities was viewed as one of its foremost features.

Below: This is possibly the first photograph ever taken of an oil-electric locomotive and a steamer on adjoining tracks. It was taken in July 1924, when Ingersoll-Rand was testing the new form of railroad power in its own yards.

into air conditioning.' And they wrote back and said, 'If we hear from you one more time on this subject, we're going to let you go. You're a madman. Air conditioning will never be successful outside of a few minor installations in the world.'"[24]

Gas Compressors

The study of various gases, and how they can be compressed to provide power, has been an ongoing effort of Ingersoll-Rand. Some gases, including oxygen and hydrogen, have posed special problems historically. These two gases required that compressors be made with special parts and specific metals. Eventually, solutions would be found for each obstacle, allowing Ingersoll-Rand to actively compete for business in this specialized field.

"It is one of the peculiarities of pneumatic terminology that air and other gases are treated as though they were entirely different substances instead of being members of the same group. However, it is true that there are differences and compressor designers often have to recognize and provide for them. There are, for instance, considerable differences in specific gravities of gases that affect their behavior during compression. ... The extent of this variation must be determined and taken into account when calculating compressor capacity."[25]

Gas engine compressors also grew in importance during the twenties. Both Rand Drill and Ingersoll-Sergeant had manufactured compressors in the 1890s that were powered by natural gas. However, supplies of natural gas were limited, and by the early 1900s, resources were running low.

"An Ingersoll-Rand bulletin of 1906 commented on 'the failure of the natural gas supply,' and visualized artificial gas compressors as an important future source of busi-

ness. ... Although the natural gas industry was to prove very fruitful of business later, the artificial gas companies were of great importance during this period."[26]

Industries involving natural gas and gasoline were financially significant for Ingersoll-Rand. When the gas-powered engine was invented, it created a large demand for fuel, prompting a greater reliance on compressors to obtain the resource.

Ingersoll-Rand recognized the opportunities provided by gas engines, and incorporated the engines for use in their own products. After about a decade of research and development, the company introduced its first direct-connected gas engine-driven compressor, the Type XG, was produced by the Painted Post plant in 1925.

Subsequent improvements in gas engine compressors in the twenties and thirties involved

the addition of an angle design, dissipation of heat generated by the gas engine, and increased power.

"Painted Post engineers gave F.W. Parsons major credit for developing the first gas-engine

Left and below: The Crawl-Air compressor at work in 1934 on the tracks of the New York Central Railroad.

A Type XVG compressor in preparation for delivery in 1934. Powered by a gas engine, the Type XVG was introduced in 1932 after considerable research by Ingersoll-Rand. It was easily moved from location to location in oil fields. The machine is a member of the Imperial Type 10 family manufactured at Painted Post.

compressors — including the XG, XOG, and XVG. Speaking on the success of the XVG at a branch managers' conference in 1938, J.J. Janzen concurred when he said, 'A fond dream and a vision of the late Mr. Parsons was realized, but on a scale even larger than he could have anticipated.'"[27]

Ingersoll-Rand grew and prospered in the twenties. In 1920, Ingersoll-Rand posted sales of $28.4 million and recorded profits of $3.9 million. By 1929, sales had blossomed to $41.7 million and profits grew to an impressive $10.7 million.

A highlight of the decade began in 1927, when Ingersoll-Rand provided Jackhamer drills for work on Mount Rushmore. The Jackhamer units were used to drill holes for explosives that helped sheer away the rock of the South Dakota mountain before the faces of George Washington, Thomas Jefferson, Abraham Lincoln and Theodore Roosevelt could be sculpted. The project, designed and supervised by Gutzon Borglum, began in 1927 and took 14 years to complete. Borglum died before the memorial was complete, and his son, Lincoln, carried on the project.

Shown here is an oversized vertical, motor-driven compressor. Designers of compressors for charging torpedoes of the Whitehead and Bliss-Leavitt types were originally held back by Navy restrictions. Eventually, a successful compressor was designed, but it was four times as heavy as the Navy specified. It was ultimately warmly received, supplying air at pressures of 1,600 to 3,000 pounds per square inch.

Two Class PRE compressors were sold to Consolidated Mining & Smelting Company in 1933 to compress ammonia synthesis gas in its fertilizer plant at Trail, British Columbia.

CHAPTER SIX

THE GREAT DEPRESSION AND WORLD WAR II

"During Keefe's presidency there was steady company growth. His business philosophy was simple and in keeping with Ingersoll-Rand tradition. He believed in building superior machinery and charging top dollar for it. He maintained that this policy would justify itself by enabling the purchaser to make more money."

— Historian C.H. Vivian

ON OCTOBER 29, 1929, a wave of panic rolled over a sea of dazed brokers, investors and bankers on Wall Street, as the stock market plummeted to an unprecedented and spectacular loss. Within an hour during the frantic day, blue chip certificates of companies like General Electric, Johns-Manville and Montgomery Ward tumbled. Black Thursday would consume the livelihoods, dreams and dignity of millions of Americans, with a cancerous attrition in the years to follow.

"Ingersoll-Rand, like every other heavy machinery manufacturer, suffered acutely during the Great Depression. The demand for large machines virtually dried up, and it became exceedingly difficult to sell even the smaller equipment."[1]

Although the Great Depression severely affected all businesses, including Ingersoll-Rand, the success of two air compressors, the Type 30, introduced in 1929, and the Type 40, introduced in 1934, helped keep many workers at their jobs during this devastating period.

The Type 30, a small, heavy-duty and efficient model invented by John LeValley, of the Painted Post facility, was the end result of more than 30 years of research and development. With the verti-

cal design inherited from the Rand side, this new model served the needs of the automotive industry, and was used for such diverse tasks as starting diesel engines, agitating milk, running air conditioning in trains and buses, tapping beer and spraying paint.

"One of the outstanding features of the Type 30 was elimination of a check valve in the discharge line — the first time this had been accomplished. Two things were responsible for it. First, a centrifugal unloader that was dependent upon compressor speed and not on the machine pumping the receiver up to cutout pressure, as was true of numerous other units. Second, the use of stainless steel valves with steel stop plate and seat. This construction was leakless, despite claims of competitors that this couldn't be true of a metal-to-metal fit. Actually the seat functioned better with use."[2]

George Doubleday's son, Chester Doubleday, got his start selling these units, recalled H. Kirk Lewis, a retired salesman.

Above: A Type 30 two-stage model from 1930, which could be set on castors for easy mobility.

and ten air-operated hoists at work. Smaller pneumatic tools abound, among them twelve clay diggers and varying numbers of drills, riveting hammers, chipping hammers, grinders, etc. All are of Ingersoll-Rand manufacture."[6]

Calyx

In the 1930s, a rodless Calyx was introduced that was well suited for deep drilling. The patent was issued to Frank Miller in 1934, who continuously made improvements to the Calyx drill for more than 20 years. These various refinements allowed the Calyx drill to be used in a variety of industries. For example, inspection holes could be drilled wide enough for geologists to actually descend within them to inspect the work first-hand. During World War II, orders for Calyx drills far outstripped supply, but demand diminished after the war.

Impactool

In 1934, Ingersoll-Rand introduced its first air Impactool, which converted torque into a series of rotary impacts. It was originally referred to as the Pott impact wrench, in honor of its inventor, Robert H. Pott, and later as the Ingersoll-Rand impact wrench. By 1948, the name impact

An engineer peers into a Calyx drill hole 5½ inches in diameter at the Tennessee Valley Authority's Norris Dam site, near Knoxville, in 1934. The eyepiece was a 6-power telescope. At the bottom of the pipe was a 500-watt lamp and just above it a mirror inclined at 45 degrees, which enabled the viewer to inspect the side walls of the hole. By turning the pipe and raising it slowly, the lower several feet of the hole could be examined to check the effectiveness of the foundation grouting procedure. Five hundred of the Calyx holes were drilled after grout had been injected through 10,000 smaller holes drilled with Ingersoll-Rand wagon drills. Also introduced at Norris Dam was the sinking of Calyx holes large enough to enable a geologist to descend to inspect the foundation rock in place. This technique was later adopted at most of the large dams built in the West by the Bureau of Reclamation.

tool was used, and in 1955, Ingersoll-Rand registered the name Impactool as a trademark.

Selling Compressors

Ingersoll-Rand began experimenting with the idea of packaged compressors in the early twenties. First considered a specialty item, the concept was to package the compressor and auxiliaries together, instead of transporting them separately to the site.

Above: The Impactool, introduced in 1934, evolved over time. A size 588 Slugger Impactool was used at the Ohio Edison Company's plant at Toronto, Ohio, in 1963 to remove nuts from 2- and 2½-inch bolts on a generator. With two men operating the Impactool, 48 bolts were removed in 75 minutes. The old method, which took eight or nine hours, was to use a steel rail weighing 120 pounds a yard, suspended from an overhead crane. One man held a long-handled wrench on a nut and five others rammed it with the rail to get the nut loose.

Left: A 534 Impactool being used to tighten steel bolts during construction of the Ford assembly plant in Mahwah, New Jersey.

Below: A 504 Impactool being used to run nuts on an air brake chamber.

In 1938, the company introduced the Type XHE compressor, which was basically an improved version of the Type XVH designed by Canadian Ingersoll-Rand in 1930.

"It had horizontally opposed cylinders with balanced forces that permitted installing it where ground conditions were unsuitable for a machine of considerable vibration. It could

1931. Doubleday was succeeded as president by Daniel C. Keefe, who had been Doubleday's assistant since 1930, and an executive vice president since 1933. Keefe had graduated from Lehigh University in 1911, and began his career with Ingersoll-Rand 18 months later. In 1926, he became a general sales manager and then worked his way up to the presidency over the following decade. Keefe presided over a prosperous time in the company, when many new and successful products were introduced. When he took the helm in 1936, sales were $27.5 million and profits were $6.4 million. When he retired in 1955, sales had increased to $145.4 million and profits more than quadrupled to $27.5 million.

"During Keefe's presidency there was steady company growth. His business philosophy was simple, and in keeping with Ingersoll-Rand tradition. He believed in building superior machinery and charging

even be mounted on a platform over water. It was of interest to oil refineries and industrial concerns with operations in tropical countries, where subsoil called for machines that did not exert reciprocating forces on the foundation."[7]

Daniel C. Keefe

In 1936, George Doubleday was elected chairman of the board, a position that had remained vacant since William L. Saunders left the post in

Above: A Type 20 portable compressor supplies air for applying stucco to one of the concrete homes in the Valley View development of Phillipsburg after World War I.

Right: The Type 30 two-stage portable compressor was offered in 1929 for outdoor service. It featured a piston displacement of 30 cubic feet per minute and could operate four paint spray guns, or one of various pneumatic tools for chipping, scaling or concrete surfacing.

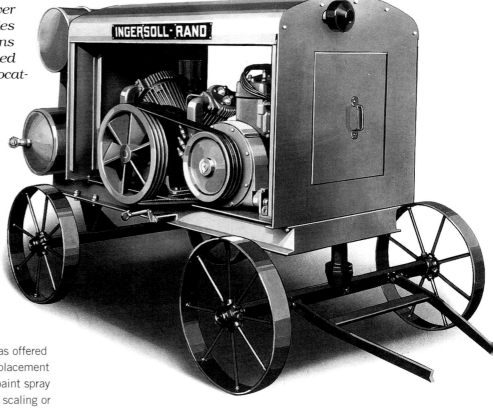

top dollar for it. He maintained that this policy would justify itself by enabling the purchaser to make more money."[8]

Keefe remained president until 1955, when he in turn was elected chairman of the board, a position he held until 1958. Keefe was a bachelor until late in his life, and he devoted the great majority of his energies to Ingersoll-Rand.

World War II

On December 7, 1941, more than 360 Japanese warplanes participated in the disastrous attack at Pearl Harbor, Hawaii, sinking or very seriously damaging five U.S. battleships and 14 smaller ships. More than 2,000 Navy personnel perished, along with 400 civilians. Within four days of the attack, the United States would declare war on Japan and her Axis partners, Italy and Germany. America joined the horrible fury of world war.

As it had during World War I, Ingersoll-Rand began an ambitious program to increase production to support the war effort. The Class PRE compressor, introduced in 1914, became strategically important during World War II. Among its solid features was the Rogler valve, which reduced costs while allowing the compressor to run faster and quieter.

Two Class PRE compressors, manufactured at the Sherbrooke factory in Canada.

"The PRE was the unquestioned leader of heavy-duty electric-driven compressors for more than 35 years. Its service life spanned two world wars and it had a brilliant record in both of them. In World War I it was heavily relied upon by the yards that built "a bridge of ships" to Europe. In World War II it was just as helpful in filling the skies with Liberator bombers. During both conflicts, when dependability counted most, the PRE was the first choice in virtually every war-contributing industry."[9]

For World War II, a different model of the ORD, which had been phased out in 1933, returned as the XRD. Manufactured at Painted Post for the war effort, XRDs were used in the ammonia oxidation process of making gunpowder.

The beginning of ammonia synthesis during World War II boosted sales dramatically for Ingersoll-Rand's high-pressure compressor business.

"It came about through the discovery around 1915 by two Germans, Fritz Haber and Karl Bosch, that one volume of nitrogen and three volumes of hydrogen would unite under certain conditions to form ammonia. This finding has had far-reaching effects. It opened the way for a sizable ammonia industry that had, up to August 1, 1962, been responsible for the sale of 369,184 total horsepower of Ingersoll-Rand high-pressure compressors for the compression of ammonia synthesis alone. This total represented 205 machines that averaged 1,900 horsepower each and exceeded the sales of any other manufacturer."[10]

The Crawl-IR drill was the successor to the wagon drill. This drill was used in 1957 in construction for the Norfolk & Western Railroad.

CHAPTER SEVEN

POST-WAR PROSPERITY

*"Most salesmen and most servicemen are gregarious. They liked
people, if they were any good. And the Ingersoll–Rand folks were good."*

— Retired Salesman H. Kirk Lewis

AFTER WORLD WAR II, the company enjoyed tremendous growth. In 1948, sales passed $100 million for the first time, reaching $117 million, with profits of $17.9 million. By 1957, sales were $205.4 million, with earnings of $36.4 million.

An aggressive sales force has always been critical to the success of Ingersoll-Rand, and the company increased the sales staff after the war. "They hired so many people right after World War II to anticipate the big increase in business," recalled H. Kirk Lewis, one of the salesmen hired at this time.[1] "We were the envy of the industry," said Joe Wiendl, retired vice president of sales. "We had the best sales force, and I think we can say we still do. We had, by far, the best sales, the best service, the best distribution."[2]

Sales representatives thoroughly understood the capabilities of their products, and were legendary in their ability to sell them. Traditionally, salesmen were taller than 6 feet, and had to wear a hat. "I was the first 5-foot, 9-inch salesman in the company," said King Cunningham, who retired in January 1995 as vice president of international marketing. "The only reason they hired me was because they knew I was going to India. Since I wasn't going to be in the United States, they took me."[3]

William Austin, retired vice president of sales for the Air Compressor Group, explained the logic behind the tradition. "Nothing wrong with short guys, but all things being equal, on your first appearance as you walk through the door, you might as well be 6 feet tall. It just gives a better appearance." One time, Austin reported to headquarters without a hat. "They told me I was better off showing up without pants than not to wear a hat."[4]

The policy remained in effect through the fifties. The suit and tie were forsaken, however, when salesmen went to mines and other job sites. "You were expected to wear whatever the mining people do, including a hard hat," Austin said. He recalled a time he was calling on a site in Arkansas.

"One day, I walked in and the [general manager of the project] grabbed me, took a pair of scissors and cut my tie. He said, 'Austin, when you call on us, dress like us.' When I'd go into a mine, I'd throw a little dust on me, run around and sweat a little bit."[5]

Even under stressful conditions, the Ingersoll-Rand salesmen managed to keep their senses of humor. An association of retired field sales and service personnel formed the G-Men's Association

Above: The Carset bit, introduced in 1946, was developed in cooperation with Carboloy Company, Inc.

in 1989. The name refers to the unusual *g* in Ingersoll-Rand before it was changed to block letters in the mid-sixties. Only employees who had been with the company long enough to remember the old logo were eligible to join the association. A 1989 issue of the association's newsletter, the *G-Rand Times,* describes what it meant to be an Ingersoll-Rand salesman.

"Most salesmen and most servicemen are gregarious. They liked people, if they were any good. And the Ingersoll-Rand folks were good. So when we hung it up, we really didn't miss the product, the phones and letters and questions from headquarters, the sales quotas, chasing parts shipments, or even getting out of a warm bed on a 15-degree morning, driving 200 miles to fix a machine that someone had forgotten to oil. We miss the people."[6]

A 1990 issue of the *G-Rand Times* is filled with affectionate stories about Ingersoll-Rand. One anecdote from Doyle Reynolds describes a classic bit of salesmanship.

"As a young salesman for Ingersoll-Rand, I was given a customer that no one seemed able to get an order from, so I decided to GO AFTER HIM.

"I approached his secretary and asked for an appointment. 'No,' she said. 'Mr. Hunter doesn't see salesmen, and besides, he's busy.' I said, 'Would you at least give him my business card? He couldn't object to just looking at my card, could he?' I gave her my card and just stood there. She stared at me wondering why I was still there. I said, 'Would it be all right if I wait until you give him my card?'

"She was a little exasperated, but she took my card in to him and returned. I stood there waiting. She asked, 'Is there anything else?' 'Yes,' I replied. 'I would like my card back.'

"'YOUR CARD BACK??!!' she almost shouted. But she went back into his office and when she came back she said, 'Mr. Hunter tore up your card and threw it in the wastebasket. Now, will there be anything else?' 'Yes,' I said. 'Those business cards cost money. Please go

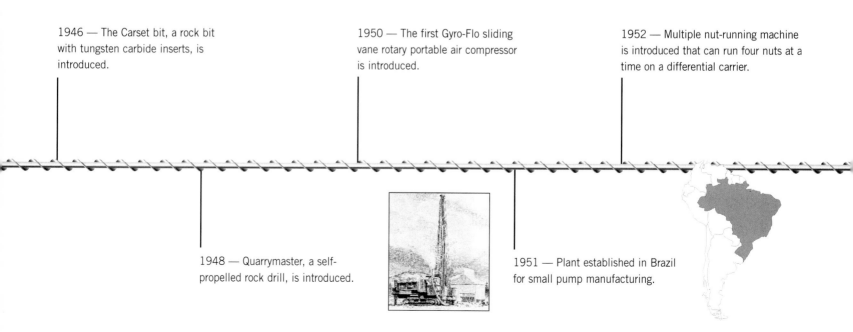

1946 — The Carset bit, a rock bit with tungsten carbide inserts, is introduced.

1950 — The first Gyro-Flo sliding vane rotary portable air compressor is introduced.

1952 — Multiple nut-running machine is introduced that can run four nuts at a time on a differential carrier.

1948 — Quarrymaster, a self-propelled rock drill, is introduced.

1951 — Plant established in Brazil for small pump manufacturing.

tell Mr. Hunter he owes me 10 cents and I would like my money.'

From Mr. Hunter's office came a booming voice, 'Tell that smart aleck I want to see him!' And from that time on, Mr. Hunter was a customer for life."[7]

A story from Jack Lehrer describes other challenges faced by sales people.

"About 35 years ago, our man in Maine, the legendary Gil Pippin, was on his beat visiting paper mills in northern Maine in mid-winter. Through some freak of fate, he knocked out the entire windshield of his company car. What does one do when the nearest town of any size, where a new windshield could be installed, is over 100 miles away? Undaunted, Gil wrapped layer upon layer of newspapers around his overcoat and hat, and off he went

Men working on the Erie Railroad in Waverly, New York, in 1948 with the help of a 3R-30 Spot-Air compressor, which powered two cribbing forks.

1954 — World's first atomic-powered submarine is equipped with Ingersoll-Rand boiler-feed pumps and compressors.

1955 — Downhole drill is introduced.

1954 — Torque-controlled angle wrenches are introduced.

January 1955 — Daniel C. Keefe elected chairman, and Donald R. Lowry becomes president.

An overhead view of a Type HHE hyper compressor, built in 1960. The Type HHE was introduced in 1949 as a heavy-duty machine for process work.

"Nothing is as important as 'positive attitude' to enhance one's growth in a corporation. ... Successful salespersons work positively and constructively with their customers and their own companies to achieve their goals. ... Negative attitude is a certain sign of failure. Positive attitude makes things happen and is a sure path to success."[15]

Air Compressors after the War

The XLE, introduced in 1947, was an advance over the XHE that had been introduced in 1938. "Before that point, we had only two quite small machines that were very old-fashioned in our product line," said David C. Garfield, president from 1981 to 1987. "Then we greatly enlarged the line so we had a complete line of machines from small to large and they were the state of the art."[16]

The XLE was used on a dam project that created Lake Casitas near Ojai, California. Retired

salesman Jack Zoeller remembered that the XLE performed admirably.

"The project manager was Fred Paterson. A small diversion tunnel was part of the project, and they needed a 150-horsepower XLE-2 compressor for the air supply. Fred wanted me to tell him what kind of foundation was required. I was told to have Winston Brothers Construction Company of Minneapolis, [the site contractor] level the ground where they wanted to put the unit, and then just place the XLE, still on its shipping skid, right there, pipe it up, connect the motor, and RUN. I passed this on to Fred.

"Several months later, Paterson called me and said they'd built a 'compressor house' for the XLE, had made all the connections, and would I come up to Casitas and start it. I sure did my homework then. Read the instruction book twice. Checked everything I could possibly think of. Finally told Fred it was ready.

A frame of a Type HHE, a heavy-duty compressor built at Painted Post, being unloaded at a dock in Great Britain.

"'Jack,' he said. 'You press the button. If that compressor walks out of that shed when it starts to run, it's YOUR compressor, not ours!'

"The XLE ran three years, the full length of the job, right there on its original shipping skid, without any grout whatsoever! The XLE was a unique design that said 'Ingersoll-Rand' loud and clear."[17]

Ingersoll-Rand continued the development of new compressor designs to meet the evolving demands of emerging new industries. In 1949, the Type HHE was introduced, a heavy-duty machine offered in four sizes. The Type HHE development was given considerable support by Ingersoll-Rand Vice President M.C. Davison, who headed the Compressor Engineering Department for many years, and credit for the unit's design is given to engineer Ray C. McAllister.

In the late 1950s, an axial compressor was added to the Ingersoll-Rand line. The patents for the new model were acquired from Read Standard Corporation in 1957, when Ingersoll-Rand purchased the rights to manufacture Read's line of blowers. With some improvements in design and engineering by Ingersoll-Rand staff, this new model, called Axi-compressor, possessed the features of both axial and rotary compressors.

The Scranton Airport

In 1947, Ingersoll-Rand sold wagon drills and portable compressors for construction of the Scranton Airport in Pennsylvania. "It was a $3.5 million job, which was a big job in those days," recalled Joe Wiendl. "Forty-eight wagon drills on the job. It was the largest wagon drill job in the world. We had all the compressors, with the exception of six that they had bought on an Army job in World War II. It made a name for me in the company."[18]

A Type HHE 5-stage compressor in 1955 at the Sherbrooke plant.

INGERSOLL–RAND has always been proud of its unusually attentive customer service, and H. Kirk Lewis recalled learning about his company's high standards when a customer complained about a cracked fronthead on a Jackhamer drill.

"In the later summer of '48, Walter Leonard arranged to have me meet 'Zip' Zimmator at his home in the city at 6 a.m., then travel with him to visit the Neversink Tunnel job that Frazier-Davis of St. Louis was doing, plus the dam job of the same name that S.A. Healy of Chicago had.

"It was on the dam project that Zip gave me my first practical lesson in what to do with customer quality complaints encountered on the job site. One of the Healy foremen had left word at the Frazier-Davis shack to come by and look at a 'defective Jackhamer' he'd just gotten off the truck from Phillipsburg that morning. 'It's got a cracked fronthead,' he said, pointing. I knelt down to scrape the paint off the 'crack,' observing sagely, 'Looks more like a hair got in the paint.'

"That was the moment when Zimmator's hand grabbed my collar and threw me three feet back on my butt. 'Lewis,' said Zip. 'Never touch anything that looks funny. If you do and it turns out it was a crack, the shops would say the customer hit it with a blunt object.' So we shipped it back.

Just another great lesson I learned while spending four days with this remarkable man. The main lesson, of course, was that the salesman and serviceman go together."[19]

The Gyro-Flo

The portable Gyro-Flo compressor, introduced in 1950, was the first portable rotary compressor on the market. After its introduction, the line was expanded to include several sizes. The Gyro-Flo was often teamed up with the Crawl-IR drill during highway construction projects. The Crawl-IR drill was a modern wagon drill that was self-propelled, completely mechanized and capable of drilling blast holes in any position. Some of the features of the Crawl-IR drill included knee-action hydraulic booms, air-powered tracks, and the ability to tow a portable air compressor.

In 1961, the Gyro-Flo was supplanted by the Spiro-Flo, a cycloidal design capable of providing greater air volumes more economically than previous portable units.

Jackdrills

During the 1950s, Jackdrills were added to the company's line of drills. The Jackdrill was a variation of the Jackhamer, and included an air-leg mount that increased maneuverability and made it possible to drill at many angles. This feature alone was a tremendous benefit to productivity.

William Mulligan, executive vice president at Ingersoll-Rand, was hired in 1952 to demonstrate rock drills. "After that program, I went into another program of demonstrating drills in underground coal mines," he said.

"When you excavate the coal from underground, you have to support the roof in some fashion. At that time, they were trying out a new method, which involved taking the strata and overlying in the open area and binding it together with bolts. So, in effect, it created a beam over the roof, or at least a more continuous beam than what had been there before. Stopers were just coming into use at that time for drilling those holes."[20]

Dust from dry drills had always been a significant problem for operators. Ingersoll-Rand found a way to eliminate dust in 1956, when it introduced the VacuJet stoper. An air jet within the drill evacuated dust through the hollow drill steel.

The Master Series

A radically different pneumatic drilling device, called the Quarrymaster, was developed, weighing a massive 21 tons. After extensive field testing in 1946 and 1947, the Quarrymaster was introduced in 1948. Engineers W.A. Morrison and O.H. Sellars both worked on some aspects of the Quarrymaster. They disagreed, however, on whether a piston drill or a hammer drill would be most effective as the principal operating device. Morrison, who is often credited with inventing the Quarrymaster, prevailed, and the piston drill was employed.

"The Quarrymaster was the first modern self-contained, portable, air-powered rock drilling plant designed for putting in large-diameter blast holes. It was complete with drill, power plant, propulsion elements and auxiliary equipment, all mounted on tractor treads. It could move overland under its own power at a rate of one mile an hour and negotiate grades of up to 30 percent."[21]

The Quarrymaster was designed so that the piston drill was powered by a portable air compressor that was part of the total power plant. The air could be used three times in each cycle, a breakthrough that dramatically reduced the amount of air previously needed to run a piston drill. The Quarrymaster met with considerable success, even though it was considered too large for most excavation assignments.

Ingersoll-Rand introduced a slightly smaller model, the Drillmaster, in 1955.

"Introduced with the Drillmaster was a revolutionary new type of drill that went down the hole as it was deepened, always drilling close to the bottom. The downhole drill as it was called, was incorporated not only in the Drillmaster, but was also adopted for use in the Quarrymaster and in the Crawlmaster, which was still to come."[22]

Morrison experimented with different bits, and eventually selected the Carset bit for the Drillmaster. Although the Drillmaster was

A drawing by Canadian artist C.B. Batchelor of a Quarrymaster drill in a Candian mining setting.

smaller than the Quarrymaster, it still weighed an impressive 16 tons. By 1958 there were Drillmaster rigs set up all around the world, from Pennsylvania to Yugoslavia. Product literature boasted that the Drillmaster was the most productive and versatile rock drill ever developed for blast-hole drilling, pointing out that it had revolutionized road building, construction and mining.

The Crawlmaster, formally introduced in 1960, was smaller yet, though it still weighed 11 tons. Among the reasons for its light weight was that it did not have its own compressor.

"The Crawlmaster represented a lot of drilling power in a considerably smaller package than either the predecessor Quarrymaster or Drillmaster. It was about one-third as much drilling plant as the QM8 that had introduced the Quarrymaster, and yet it could put down

The durability of Ingersoll-Rand air compressors and drills made them ideal for tough desert conditions, such as this 1977 Middle Eastern project.

CHAPTER EIGHT

ACQUISITIONS AND DIVERSIFICATION

Mr. Johnson and Mr. Hopton adopted a program with several aspects, one being to acquire other companies. We were reasonably successful at that."

— David C. Garfield

WITH ROBERT JOHNSON as CEO and Lester Hopton as president, Ingersoll-Rand underwent a significant period of expansion. "Prior to that time, we were really in a mode of biding our time, waiting for exactly what, I don't know," said David C. Garfield, who was then vice president and would become president from 1981 to 1987.

"But the presumption was there would be a post-war depression duplicating events following World War I. ... Around 1956 or so, we were the second company in the Fortune 500 *survey with regard to profitability. Our profit after tax was something like 18 percent, and this was when income tax was over 50 percent.*

"This new management felt this was great, but the world was passing us by and probably a few more years of that and we might have some irreversible difficulties with our competition or we might be taken over by other larger companies. Mr. Johnson and Mr. Hopton adopted a program with several aspects, one being to acquire other companies. We were reasonably successful at that."[1]

Garfield's assessment of the success of the strategy was something of an understatement. Between 1961 and 1966, Ingersoll-Rand acquired eight major companies and boosted sales from $204.9 million to $437.6 million.

Aldrich Pump Company

The first company acquired under the bold program was Aldrich Pump Company. On May 25, 1961, Ingersoll-Rand acquired all outstanding common stock of Aldrich in exchange for treasury shares of the company. The affiliation consisted of a pooling of interests for accounting purposes. Historian C.H. Vivian pointed out that Aldrich would not compete against the Cameron line, which Ingersoll-Rand had purchased in 1909.

"Aldrich pumps complement rather than compete with the Cameron line. They consist chiefly of specialized high-pressure reciprocating pumps and hydraulic auxiliaries. ... They are used for continuous work in oil field, chemical and metal working applications."[2]

Millers Falls Company

On June 15, 1962, Ingersoll-Rand acquired the Millers Falls Company, a manufacturer of

Above: An air impact wrench introduced by the Professional Tool Group in 1983 for the automotive market.

hand and universal electric tools, by purchasing the company's outstanding stock. The Millers Falls acquisition added metal-cutting saws and precision tools, for both home and industrial use, to the Ingersoll-Rand line.

The Millers Falls Company was incorporated in 1868 by H.L. Pratt. Originally, it was a general manufacturing firm, utilizing power from the Millers Falls River in Massachusetts. The company was an important supplier of machinists' precision tools during World War II. After the war, Millers Falls developed tools geared toward home use, capitalizing on the new trend of do-it-yourself projects.

D. Wayne Hallstein, president from 1967 to 1974, recalled that Ingersoll-Rand was specifically interested in acquiring an electric tool company.

"That's the only one that would even talk. It was an inexpensive purchase, and it was a poor investment in the long run. They were pretty good in their engineering. They were the first ones to come out with shock-proof electric drills and tools, but they were expensive and heavier, and I guess they didn't have a good distribution setup in various stores."[3]

The Aldrich Pump Company's factory in Allentown, Pennsylvania, shortly after it was acquired by Ingersoll-Rand in 1961.

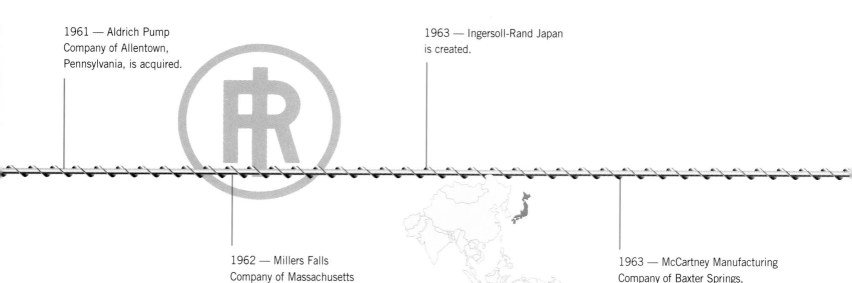

1961 — Aldrich Pump Company of Allentown, Pennsylvania, is acquired.

1963 — Ingersoll-Rand Japan is created.

1962 — Millers Falls Company of Massachusetts is acquired.

1963 — McCartney Manufacturing Company of Baxter Springs, Kansas, is acquired.

The Aldrich Pump facility was expanded and modernized after the acquisition, as this aerial photograph shows.

James O'Dell, vice president of technology, recalled that Ingersoll-Rand had tried, without success, to buy Black & Decker, and so purchased Millers Falls instead.

"We didn't put any money into it. We didn't put any people into it, which was really too bad because Millers Falls had the patent on the double-insulated electric tool, which was really a strong market presence. ... It got to the point where we were really going to have to put a lot of money in it, develop all new product lines. We just decided to get out of the business."[4]

McCartney Manufacturing Company

McCartney Manufacturing Company became a wholly owned subsidiary of Ingersoll-Rand in May 1963 in an exchange of stock and pooling of financial interests. This acquisition added high-pressure equipment for the petrochemical and refining industries to Ingersoll-Rand product lines. McCartney Manufacturing Company was founded in 1944 by Joseph A. McCartney. As McCartney's health deteriorated in the early sixties, he opted to ensure a future for his company by selling it.

1964 — Pendleton Tool Industries Inc. of Los Angeles is acquired.

1964 — Lee-Norse Company of Charleroi, Pennsylvania, is acquired.

1966 — Lawrence Manufacturing Company of Seattle is acquired.

1964 — Southwest Industries of Houston is acquired.

1964 — Improved Machinery Inc. of Nashua, New Hampshire, is acquired.

"After considerable investigation and thought, he decided that Ingersoll-Rand best met the standards he had established and perhaps would follow the course he had chartered. Having made his decision, he contacted Ingersoll-Rand officials, found them receptive, and terms of transfer were agreed upon."[5]

Pendleton Tool Industries

Pendleton Tool Industries was the next company to become a wholly owned subsidiary of Ingersoll-Rand when it was acquired February 28, 1964. The agreement between Pendleton and Ingersoll-Rand provided one share of Ingersoll-Rand common stock for every three shares of Pendleton stock. Pendleton had a diverse range of products, including mechanics' service tools, plastic products, metal tool boxes, special equipment for the aircraft industry, and electronic and guided missile industry parts.

The company began as a blacksmith operation in 1907, run by Alonzo Plomb, Jacob Weninger and Charles H. Williams. Plomb withdrew about 1915, and Weninger and Williams continued, aided by capital supplied by William Zeigler, who handled the office and administrative duties. When Zeigler died suddenly in 1917, Williams induced John H. Pendleton, a manufacturers' representative, to enter the firm as a partner. His son, Morris B. Pendleton, was president when the company was acquired by Ingersoll-Rand.

Original blacksmith shop at ninth and Towne streets, Los Angeles, where Pendleton Tool Industries, Inc., began business in 1907. This picture from 1916 shows some of the hand-crafted chisels and punches in the foreground and the entire staff of employees. Left to right: Joseph Berner, Joseph Matz and Joseph Weninger. When Weninger retired in the 1950s, he was general foreman of Pendleton's Industrial Tools Plant in Huntington Park, California.

Above: Air-powered screwdrivers were among the items manufactured by Ingersoll-Rand after Pendleton Tool Industries was acquired.

Right: In 1960, Southwest Industries, Inc. installed four Type HHE compressors for service by the Continental Oil Company in Louisiana.

John Pendleton died in 1924, and through the remainder of the decade and into the next, the company struggled, forced to sell stock to stay in business. Pendleton grew considerably during the fifties. "This growth was not accomplished of course, without considerable effort," noted Vivian.

"Pendleton recalls that while he was on a trip during that period, someone placed a sign outside his office door, which he says will always remain there. It reads: 'Anybody who considers work a pleasure will have a hell of a lot of fun in this organization.'"[6]

Hallstein recalled that Pendleton was purchased in an effort to broaden the line of tools offered by Ingersoll-Rand. But, he said, Pendleton "had an inferior manufacturing set-up. We poured a lot of money into them. We just couldn't seem to get them back in line."[7] The company was sold to The Stanley Works in 1984.

"We got out of that kind of tool business," said William Wearly, CEO from 1967 to 1980. "But we owned it for several years. It was in Los Angeles. They made Proto tools, which were very good wrenches, that sort of thing."[8]

Southwest Industries

On April 30, 1964, Ingersoll-Rand acquired Southwest Industries, based in Houston with branch offices in Tulsa, New Orleans, Calgary, and Mexico City. Southwest Industries developed equipment to produce inert gas, and installed packaged gas compressors on portable skids for gas lift, booster service, pressure maintenance, and main-line pumping. Units manufactured by the company included cooling systems, air starting equipment, and lubricating, scrubbing and automatic control systems.

Beginning in 1959, Southwest developed equipment for producing inert gas. In addition to packaging compressors, Southwest engineered and built complete stations in oil fields, including offshore platforms and barges.[9]

William Wearly and Lee-Norse

Arthur L. Lee created Lee-Norse in 1936 with the intention of developing shuttle cars and machinery for coal mines. When E.M. Arentzen joined Lee-Norse in 1940, Norse was added to the company name to reflect Arentzen's Norwegian heritage. In 1940, Arentzen bought out Lee and gained control of the company. Until the early 1950s, Lee-Norse's main activity was manufacturing shuttle cars and converting mine machinery running on tracks to trackless mounting.[10]

When Ingersoll-Rand acquired Lee-Norse, the company also got Wearly, the former CEO of competitor Joy Manufacturing Company, both manufacturers of underground coal mining equipment. Wearly, who would become chairman of Ingersoll-Rand from 1967 to 1980, had begun working at Joy in 1937, after he graduated from Purdue University.

Wearly started in Joy's engineering department in 1942, and was made service manager. "I virtually ran the company," he said.

"Now, this sounds funny, but the president didn't run it. He was just an investor. ... My boss, the executive vice president, ran the War Production Board for the mining industry. He was totally busy. He would come home every weekend and I would sit with him Saturday and Sunday and decide what to do the next week. I was running the company with people making five times as much money as I was."[11]

During World War II, Joy became an important company because coal was needed to power factories and to make steel, Wearly said. "I just became an important person in kind of a little job, and all of a sudden I was made vice president of Joy. We began expanding, we got into the compressor business and that's how I came to know Ingersoll-Rand."[12]

The Lee-Norse exhibit at the Coal Show in Cleveland, only a few days after the purchase of the company by Ingersoll-Rand had been announced, in May 1964.

Joy began marketing turbo compressors, a departure from the reciprocating compressors that dominated the market. "Ingersoll was far and away number one in reciprocating compressors. They were so far in the lead that they didn't want to look at the turbo compressor, even though they had a division that made turbo compressors," Wearly said. "They used the turbo compressor for gas and other things, but not for compressed air."[13]

Theodore H. Black, who was general manager of the turbo products division from 1967 to 1972, and became CEO in 1988, recalled that turbo compressors were less profitable than other products.

"It's a more complicated machine than most of the machines our people were dealing with, but unfortunately it never really made the kind of money that some of the other businesses did. There was always a great deal of emphasis on construction in the company. Models of our founding rock drills are sitting outside the board room.

"It was a business that was not new because blast furnaces have been around for-

ever. That's a turbo product. And we populated the world with these blowers for blast furnaces. Big, slow machines. But we didn't put the research and development and spend the money on turbo products that were spent on the more profitable lines. Ingersoll-Rand had, in addition to construction and mining, a premier position in the air compressor business. And the air compressor business, for all practical purposes, was a reciprocating compressor.

"It [the turbo compressor] was a machine of the future that wasn't sufficiently emphasized because the company was oriented to the profitability that was associated with some of the other lines."[14]

Wearly said his former company took advantage of this competitive edge.

"Joy put on the market a turbo compressor for compressed air, and Ingersoll-Rand just refused to look at it and they wouldn't even talk about it. We were moving up in the marketplace, and I had spent a considerable amount of money to do this. It really stretched Joy, and I was funding it out of the coal-mining machinery business. By 1960, the coal-mining machinery business went into a slump, so it was straining us to keep putting this money into compressors. But I kept doing it and the board finally fired me. I got fired from Joy in 1962, after having been CEO for six years."[15]

After Wearly was fired, he tried to form his own company by merging three existing companies, Lee-Norse, Goodman Manufacturing Company and Galis Electric & Machine Company. "All of a sudden," he said. "I got a call from Ingersoll-Rand. They said, 'We'd like to see you.'"[16]

Hallstein, a future company president, recalled that CEO Johnson was eager to hire Wearly.

"Bob [Johnson] told him to come to New York because he wanted to talk to him right away. And so he hired him as vice president. Eventually he was made executive vice president and given the rock drill and portable compressor divisions, which he was very familiar with from his days at Joy."[17]

But there was an obstacle to cross before Wearly could join Ingersoll-Rand, as Wearly explained.

"I went over to see Bob Johnson, the chairman. And he said, 'We want you to come work with us. You can write your own ticket.' It was obvious they thought I'd done a pretty good job even though the Joy board didn't think so. So I said, 'Well, right now I'm tied up merging these coal-mining companies.' And they said, 'Well, put them together and we'll take the whole thing. We'll take you and the coal-mining machine companies.'"[18]

The Lee-Norse Division offered a renowned line of underground continuous miners. The cutter design on this low-seam coal miner made it possible to smoothly and quickly rip through coal seams as low as 30 inches.

Right: A pair of three-section Weldrum log barkers. The acquisition of Improved Machinery made Ingersoll-Rand a force in the production of pulp industry machinery.

Below: Three freight cars of pneumatic filters built by Improved Machinery Inc. in 1904. The company's first factory is in the background. The tower rising to the left was the office that housed the two-man drafting department.

Unfortunately, the Justice Department ruled that Ingersoll-Rand could not acquire all three companies, as it would be an antitrust violation that would reduce competition and give Ingersoll-Rand an unfair advantage.[19]

In reaching a compromise with the federal government, Ingersoll-Rand withdrew its proposal for certain parts of Goodman and completely dropped the proposal for Galis. On May 6, 1964, Ingersoll-Rand acquired Lee-Norse. "We brought them in, and, oh, they made money. It was beautiful, even by Ingersoll-Rand standards," Wearly said.[20]

Wearly, who was a vice president of Ingersoll-Rand at the time, was elected president and CEO of Lee-Norse. Arentzen, who had been president of Lee-Norse, became chairman of that board.

Improved Machinery, Inc.

Acquired May 21, 1964, Improved Machinery, Inc., of Nashua, New Hampshire, became a wholly owned subsidiary that manufactures equipment for pulp and paper processing and plastic molding.

The company began as Improved Paper Machinery Company, established by Charles and Walter Morey in 1900. In 1901, it acquired the Bates Machine Company. Vivian discovered that the company produced torpedo parts for the Navy during World War II.

"This called for a new kind of manufacturing procedure, and the erection and equipping of another building. Three shifts a day became the normal program. The company was the first in the area to employ female machine tool operators, a lead that was followed by others. The Army-Navy 'E' was presented to the firm in August 1943."[21]

When the war ended, Improved Paper Machinery Corporation converted back to previous manufacturing lines. In 1953, it became Improved Machinery, Inc. The acquisition positioned Ingersoll-Rand as a major supplier for the pulp and paper industry, with products ranging from pulp presses to chip dischargers to fiber treating equipment.

Dick Johnson, executive director of public affairs, remembered that one asset acquired with the company was a yacht called *Suzie Q*. Ingersoll-Rand sold the boat to a man in Houston, but the boat never reached its destination.

"They were going to steam it down toward Florida over into Texas. And the guy bought it in July or whatever, and he insisted it be delivered in August or September. Now the crew from up in Maine refused to take the boat down because the hurricanes were coming. But this guy was adamant that he was going to have it there. To make a long story short, they flew a crew up from Texas and they started steaming off with the yacht down and around the coast. They got into some hellish storms, terrible storms. They got as far as Florida and brought it in some place outside of Fort Lauderdale. They convinced the buyer they shouldn't go any further, at least until the hurricane season was over. And the thing caught on fire and burned to the ground."[22]

Lawrence Manufacturing Company

Ingersoll-Rand acquired the Lawrence Manufacturing Company of Seattle in August 1966. The acquisition included Alkirk, Inc., which held patents for Alkirk Tunnel Borers. James C. Lawrence continued as president of Lawrence after it became a wholly owned subsidiary of Ingersoll-Rand.

A compaction baffle filter under construction in Nashua, New Hampshire. The filter, which removes residual chemicals from pulp, featured decreased power requirements, size and installation costs.

A combination seven-stage axial-flow compressor with the top halves of the casings removed. The assembly was built in 1962 as the main air supply source for a tonnage oxygen plant. Driven by a 9,000-horsepower motor, it has capacity to discharge 53,330 cubic feet per minute of inlet air at a final pressure of 93 pounds per square inch.

CHAPTER NINE

ENGINEERED FOR GROWTH

"Every month, he would write, longhand, maybe 500 notes to different department heads all over the company, telling them, 'This doesn't look good, let's do something about it, let me know what you're doing,'"

— William Wearly, describing the hands-on approach of Lester Hopton

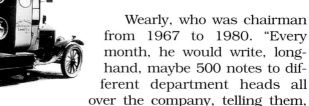

PRESIDENT LESTER C. Hopton and Chairman Robert Johnson would often invite members of the sales force to lunch, in an effort to learn more about the company. Though it was an honor to dine with the company's top executives, salesmen would often leave hungry, as William Austin recalled.

"Soup to begin with. And while you were trying to eat the soup, Mr. Johnson was asking questions and Mr. Hopton was eating his soup. So your soup got cold and you never got a chance to eat it. Then they'd take it away and bring the next course. This time, Mr. Johnson would eat and Mr. Hopton would ask you questions. You never got a thing to eat. They'd take that away and bring you ice cream, and one of them would ask you questions and one of them would eat. The damned ice cream would be melting all over the place, and you'd go back hungry as hell."[1]

The story reflects the hands-on approach that is characteristic of the two men who ran the company through the first half of the sixties, a time of tremendous growth and prosperity for Ingersoll-Rand.

Hopton prided himself on knowing what was going on in every department, recalled William Wearly, who was chairman from 1967 to 1980. "Every month, he would write, longhand, maybe 500 notes to different department heads all over the company, telling them, 'This doesn't look good, let's do something about it, let me know what you're doing.'"[2]

Sometimes, employees were reluctant to brief him on the latest developments, especially if they involved complicated sales deals that had not yet been finalized. Hopton, along with many Ingersoll-Rand employees, rode the Jersey Central Ferry, commuting to the 11 Broadway main office. Salesman Gene Miller recalled that sales people would sometimes hide from Hopton so they wouldn't have to update him on projects for which Ingersoll-Rand had bid. "Most of them had cultivated the captain and/or chief engineer of the ferry, so they spent many mornings crossing on the Hudson River in the engine room or the wheelhouse. Anything to avoid Les!"[3]

Divisionalization

Johnson and Hopton prepared the company to begin a transition into a divisionalized struc-

---

Above: Engineering for the future, an early truck-mounted air compressor.

Company directors at Painted Post during a board meeting October 5, 1960. Left to right: E.E. Teach, Painted Post plant manager; Directors G. Chester Doubleday, E. Raymond Sheerin, Richard L. Carpenter, Augustus S. Blagden Jr., Robert L. Loeb, Edward J. Smith, Lester C. Hopton, Edward J. Parish, Robert H. Johnson, M.C. Davison and John H. Phipps.

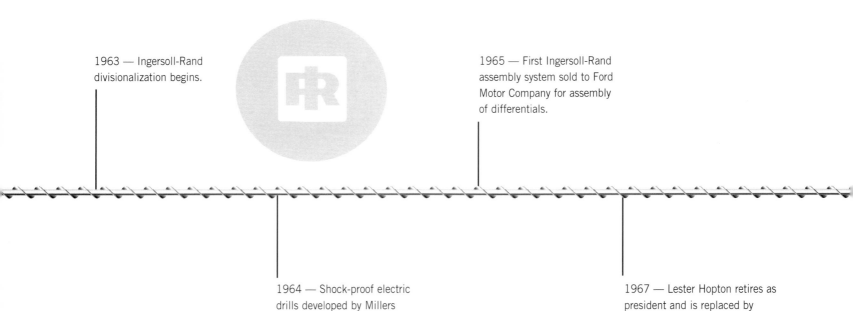

1963 — Ingersoll-Rand divisionalization begins.

1965 — First Ingersoll-Rand assembly system sold to Ford Motor Company for assembly of differentials.

1964 — Shock-proof electric drills developed by Millers Falls subsidiary

1967 — Lester Hopton retires as president and is replaced by D. Wayne Hallstein.

ture, in which the large, centralized company was divided into groups based on products. Theodore H. Black, CEO from 1988 to 1993, explained why the system was put in place.

"General management was started in 1964 under Bob Johnson. Call it a Harvard invention. In the old days, you would have a man who was manager of a plant. He would build these machines at a cost and somebody in New York would decide the sales price. Then it became the vogue, heavily talked and written about in the University of Chicago and Harvard and the Wharton School, to organize into divisions.

"You would have a guy heading the division, called the general manager or president. And you formulated similar things under him. Just air compressors for example, or just pumps. And if you got more refined, there would be certain types of pumps. The division general man-

Chairman Robert H. Johnson, left, and President Lester C. Hopton, at the annual meeting of Ingersoll-Rand stockholders held at the new Research Center near Princeton, New Jersey, in April 1966.

1967 — Robert Johnson retires as CEO and is replaced by William Wearly.

1968 — First of new Centac line of 100-psi centrifugal air compressors shipped.

1968 — Ingersoll-Rand acquires The Torrington Company.

1968 — Whisperized portable compressors are introduced.

church together. In fact, most of the people I associated with were union. We hunted and played golf and so forth. We didn't have enough capacity. We were always stretching to get more and more out.

"Of course, you didn't have very good systems back then. Everything was manual, so you did everything by sheer force. It was typi-

cally a six-day work week, and on Sunday morning, you'd find that most of the supervisors, certainly the foremen, were catching up on their paperwork. It was a way of life. You worked very hard. But it was different back then. People put in a lot more hours of work, but they also played a lot harder than they do today, and they hit the bars at night."[12]

But in the sixties, the company's facilities in Painted Post, Phillipsburg and Athens all suffered some union difficulties, said David Garfield, executive vice president at the time, and president from 1981 to 1987.

"All three were organized. It certainly wasn't a lot of fun. We had at least one strike in Phillipsburg that was just not very nice at all, lasting six to eight months. ... We didn't have any violence, but I think it is something that may still affect attitudes there a little bit after 35 years. We have come around to a situation now where we have so many plants that aren't really organized. The only one I can think of off hand that is really organized is the one at Torrington. We have at least a dozen plants that are not unionized, so it's a little bit different. Hopefully we can treat the people in the plant the same way we treat our salary workers and have them feel they are working for a good outfit that treats them fairly and where they have good opportunity. I believe that is the case."[13]

Unions nearly shut down the Painted Post plant in the sixties, said Popejoy, general manager of the compressor division at the time.

"Due to some severe strikes and poor management, difficult labor relations had developed. The plant had a relatively bad reputation with top management of the company, and there were periods from the mid-sixties on when business was really bad. They moved all

Left: This valveless downhole drill achieved fast penetration with high-pressure air.

Athens, Phillipsburg, Painted Post and Easton were the first of many manufacturing plants that Ingersoll-Rand would have in the United States. Today, Ingersoll-Rand facilities can be found in California, Colorado, Connecticut, Georgia, Illinois, Indiana, Iowa, Kansas, Kentucky, Maryland, Michigan, Nebraska, New Hampshire, New Jersey, New York, North Carolina, North Dakota, Ohio, Pennsylvania, South Carolina, Tennessee, Texas, Virginia and Washington state. Pictured left to right: F.J. Stewart, W.A. Heinze, G.E. Hancock, D.J. Burnett, C.H. Swanteson, F.W. Sultan, W.T. Alderson, D.J. Feaster, M.W. Terrill, H.E. Bolton, J.J. Janzen, R.L. Olund, M.W. Thomassen, A.H. Beard, R.G. Kaminski, F.J. Wetzel, R.C. Behrens, R.D. MacDuff, and L.L. Lauver.

the portable products out, and the air compressor products.

"Eventually, we were able to turn it around and make money. A lot of years when things were tough we were able to put some money back in for equipment or machines."[14]

Direct Distributors

In the sixties, the company began acquiring distributors so it could sell directly to customers. "That was the start of our ascent to number one in the products we sold in the marketplace," said William Mulligan, who put the plan in motion. "It was a great departure from the way we had done business."[15]

"The situation with our distributors at that time was one of facing increasing competition from the direct sale of product by one of our major competitors, Gardner Denver. Gardner Denver had set up a company in New Jersey and was

selling directly to the contractors instead of going through the distributor. This allowed them to sell the product at a lower price. It put a lot of pressure on our distributors."[16]

Over the course of the decade, Ingersoll-Rand purchased Thalman Equipment Company in New York, Henry H. Meyer Company in Baltimore, Loggers and Contractors in Portland, Oregon, and Bay City's Equipment Company in San Francisco, among others, Mulligan recalled.

"It was a market strategy that took us from being an important player to being the unquestioned leader in the products we sold."[17]

New Products

Though acquisitions fueled a great deal of Ingersoll-Rand's expansion during the sixties, the company continued to develop innovative products.

"In 1961 the principle of multiple-tool opera-tion, previously applied to pneumatic tools, was extended to rock drills by grouping several Downhole drills served by a single backhead. First called the gang drill or Gangamatic, it was later rechristened the Magnum."[18]

The Magnum drill was first used in New York City to drill holes for hydraulic elevators at Lincoln Center.

The company continued to innovate in com-pressor design, focusing on smaller models with greater capacity. The *1965 Annual Report* empha-sized that air compressors were an integral part of Ingersoll-Rand's success.

"Compressed air power systems are, next to electricity, the most widely used power sys-tems in industry and have almost as broad a field of application. Ingersoll-Rand is a world

A Canadian Ingersoll-Rand centrifugal compressor working for the Trans-Canada pipeline in Cabri, Saskatchewan, in 1963.

Right: Whisperized portable compressors with low noise emissions allowed work crews to proceed almost unnoticed at New York's famed Lincoln Center for the Performing Arts in 1977.

leader in manufacturing vital components of power systems for supplying and using compressed air. As long as the company maintains this solid position here and abroad, which it is now organized and equipped to do, it should benefit from the steady growth of demand for air power in both the developed and underdeveloped areas of the globe."[19]

An Attempt at Computerization

In the sixties, Ingersoll-Rand found that modernizing some aspects of the business with a computer system was not an easy process. D. Wayne Hallstein, who would become president in 1967, was one of the first to bring computers to Ingersoll-Rand. "I happened to be the first guy to put a computer into the Athens plant and I damn near lost my job," he said. "The whole thing just blew up, and customers were screaming at me."[20] Tired of the aggravation, Hallstein telephoned the chairman of IBM, Tom Watson.

"Surprisingly enough, he answered the phone. His secretary didn't. I told him who I was and what my problem was, and I said, 'I'm going to throw the thing out in the middle of the street and let the newspapers know if you can't fix this thing. You have one week.' 'Oh gosh,' he said. 'I can't do it in one week, but give me two.' And I agreed. The next morning there must have been half a dozen vice presidents from IBM in my office. Watson must have really chewed them out and told them not to come back until its fixed. Well, they didn't fix it. The thing kept getting worse and worse. So I said, 'Your two weeks are up. Out.' ... Monday morning we were back in business the old way."[21]

Global Sensitivity

Ingersoll-Rand has a proud tradition of responding to concerns about the environment, dwindling energy supplies and pollution. At the end of 1969, the company made an explicit commitment to produce products that were environmentally friendly.

As one response, the company made important strides in the reduction of noise pollution. Compressors were often used in urban areas, and the noises produced by the machines were of increasing concern. In 1968, Ingersoll-Rand introduced a new line of "Whisperized" portable compressors that reduced noise by 90 percent. The fight against noise pollution continued with the introduction of the LLE "Air Cube" reciprocating compressor. New and quieter compressors continue to be introduced. They were used during construction at Lincoln Center for the Performing Arts in New York in 1977.

On another front, Ingersoll-Rand products have helped solve a growing landfill problem, by contributing to a revolutionary waste disposal system. In 1970, an Ingersoll-Rand compressor was the power source that supplied air for the first odorless garbage disposal plant in St.

Above: William Wearly, chairman of Ingersoll-Rand from 1967 to 1980.

Right: D. Wayne Hallstein was president of Ingersoll-Rand from 1967 to 1974.

University. He recalled that he accepted the job even though a recruiter warned him that it might not be permanent.

"The recruiter came in and said, 'Business hasn't been very good lately and this may be a temporary job. But in 1940, that was the only offer I got, even though I was in the top 10 percent of my graduating class. That temporary job ended in 1986, 46 years later, when I retired from the board of directors."[23]

Hallstein started out in the Pneumatic Tool Division before joining the Army as a reserve second lieutenant in April 1942. When he was discharged as major in 1946, he returned to Ingersoll-Rand as a sales engineer. He moved through the ranks and became vice president in charge of the Tool & Hoist Division worldwide in 1960. In 1962, Hallstein became executive vice president, and in 1963 he was elected to the board of directors.

Wearly, hired as vice president in 1964, was also a Purdue graduate. He was the first

Petersburg, Florida. The plant was designed to convert waste into non-odorous soil compost.

New Leadership

Hopton retired as president in 1966, and Johnson retired as chairman in 1967. Wearly succeeded Johnson as chairman of the board, a position he held until 1980. Hallstein succeeded Hopton as president, remaining in this position until 1974.

Hallstein and Wearly worked closely together, dividing responsibilities. Hallstein was in charge of sales and personnel, while Wearly had responsibility for research and finances. "We worked pretty hand in glove," said Hallstein. "We always worked together. It really wasn't a boss and subordinate type of relationship."[22]

Hallstein was hired in 1940, after receiving a mechanical engineering degree from Purdue

Ingersoll-Rand CEO who did not rise through company ranks. "When he first came in, you felt resentment about it," admitted Hallstein. "But he was the kind of guy that after a while just sort of works in with everybody."[24]

King Cunningham, retired vice president of international marketing, remembered that Wearly was "a breath of fresh air because he had done a lot of work in Russia for Joy and overseas marketing. So he brought an international flavor to Ingersoll-Rand."[25] Wearly had a down-to-earth style that made him popular with employees and their wives.

"My wife thought he was the greatest guy because he used to travel and when he'd come, he'd bring his wife and he'd always want to party with local customers. When I was running Holland, Wearly came over twice. A couple of times we had parties at our house. Bill was great. When he got back to the states, his secretary ordered gold pins for the ladies, for the local managers' wives. Here's a great big actual gold pin, about one ounce of gold, with my wife's initials on it. You can imagine when a wife gets this from the chairman of the company. ... It took him two minutes to say to his secretary, 'Her initials are CSC,' but my wife for the rest of her life thought Wearly was great."[26]

Wearly doesn't recall any resentment from other employees when he was given the top job in the company. "It sure wasn't evident," he said. "They knew me. I had the opportunity of coming in the construction and mining field where I knew more about it than many of them did, and they accepted me for that reason. ... And the man that became president the same time I was made chairman and CEO, Wayne Hallstein, he clearly could have been the guy who would be upset that this outsider came in, but he was my president and I'll tell you, he was the most loyal guy you have ever seen."[27]

Hallstein would remain president until 1974, and Wearly would remain chairman until 1980. Together, the two men would lead the company through a remarkable period of acquisition and growth.

Wearly and Hallstein were younger than their predecessors when they took office, and they gave the company new vigor. "Bill was not yet 52, and Wayne was 48," noted Garfield. "So it was a lot different than having two middle-sixties guys running the place. They of course had their ideas, although we continued pretty much along the same line of trying to make some further acquisitions and trying to build up our business on a worldwide mode."[28]

The men began their leadership on a vigorous note, and their comments in the 1967 *Annual Report* were filled with confidence.

"We think 1968 will be a good year for the Ingersoll-Rand Company. Most economists seem to be forecasting sizable increases in economic activity both here in the United States and abroad. Capital spending by U.S. industry is forecast to be up between 4 percent and 8 percent. If this economic growth materializes, we are hopeful of continuing the increases in sales and earnings which have characterized the past few years. Our company is now well over twice the size it was at the start of this decade."[29]

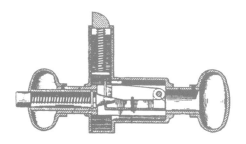

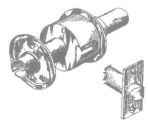

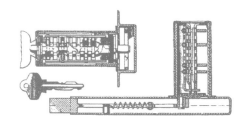

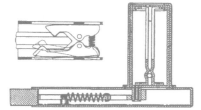

The Torrington Company manufactures a full range of bearings available in thousands of different sizes, for use in automotive, agricultural, construction and industrial markets. In the background, locks and other door hardware joined the extensive Ingersoll-Rand product list with the acquisition of Schlage Lock Company.

CHAPTER TEN

TWO REMARKABLE ACQUISITIONS

*"[Marron] Kendrick set out to find a partner that would be compatible,
that would be in a similar enough business, but not necessarily in the
hardware business, and somebody we could all get along with. We
have gotten along with Ingersoll-Rand some 20 years now."*

— David Lasier, retired president of the
Door Hardware Group

INGERSOLL-RAND entered new fields in 1968 and 1974 with two important acquisitions, destined to provide lasting benefits for the company. On October 10, 1968, Ingersoll-Rand acquired The Torrington Company, a highly successful manufacturer of bearings and components. On April 16, 1974, Ingersoll-Rand purchased Schlage Lock Company, a leader in the field of locks and other door equipment. In both acquisitions, Ingersoll-Rand strayed from its core business of drills and air compressors, and in both cases, the acquisitions have proved to be both enduring and profitable.

Torrington

The Torrington Company was already 102 years old when Ingersoll-Rand acquired it in an exchange of stock in 1968. Torrington began its successful life as the Excelsior Needle Company, which manufactured needles for the recently invented sewing machine. Excelsior's mechanically-produced needles were uniform in size and shape, making them a vast improvement over hand-forged needles. The Excelsior Company grew rapidly, and by 1880 it employed 75 people. By 1886 it employed 125 workers. In 1891, the company began manufacturing spokes for bicycle wheels. In 1898, the Excelsior Needle Company was purchased by The Torrington Company of Maine, which had been formed a mere two days earlier. "It was now a major part of a new corporation recapitalized for $3 million under the new Maine holding company."[1]

The company continued to grow, supplying surgical needles during World War I and wire wheels for automobiles following the war. In 1905, Torrington purchased the Domestic Sewing Machine Company of Newark, New Jersey, an acquisition that included a carpet-sweeper manufacturer. After World War II, it acquired Domestic Electric Manufacturing Company, of Worcester, Massachusetts, which manufactured vacuum cleaners. But it was a small ball bearing business purchased from Splitdorf Electrical in 1912 that would lead the company to its greatest success. In 1933, research engineer E.K. Brown patented the needle bearing. "It was the spark that finally led Torrington to nail down a niche in the world of bearings."[2]

Brown's idea was to create a one-piece cup to contain a circle of needle rollers with shaped ends. Thin needle rollers were already being used "loose" in certain applications, but they

---

Above: The Torrington Company originally manufactured sewing machine needles.

Above: In the twenties, workers grind ball bearings in the Standard plant at Torrington.

Right: This cross-section illustrates the components of a needle bearing designed to help customers save both space and weight.

were hard to handle. Brown knew that hundreds of industrial concerns would use self-contained needle bearings.[3]

Needle bearings were to play an important role during World War II. Most went to aircraft.

"The big B-29s were most spectacular in the public eye, and hidden from that eye, some 2,000 Torrington bearings were at work in each such Super Fortress. ... The word 'aircraft' means not only the planes themselves, but instruments and component mechanisms, such as linkage systems for operating ailerons, rudders, flaps, doors, and so on. Ensuring proper functioning, needle bearings were right at home at these junction points and reduced wear to a minimum, cutting maintenance."[4]

Torrington also supplied needles to sew parachutes, gas masks and cartridge belts, as well as surgical needles. For the company's contributions to World War II, it was awarded the coveted Army-Navy "E" Award.

Al Nixon, president of Torrington, joined the organization in 1963. "The first 10 years I was here, all we worked on

1866 — Excelsior Needle Company created.

1905 — Torrington purchases Domestic Sewing Machine Company and enters vacuum cleaner business.

1898 — Excelsior purchased by The Torrington Company of Maine.

1933 — Research engineer E.K. Brown patents the needle bearing.

was what plants needed to be added next, and how could we increase capacity. Business was booming! We were just coming out of a recession in 1961 and 1962, and so the name of the game was very much oriented toward marketing."[5] Nixon was appointed general manager of Torrington's Special Products Division in 1974, and in 1983 he became vice president and general manager of the Needle Bearings Division.

In 1972, Torrington acquired Commercial Sciences Corporation, manufacturer of various items, including Wesco-brand stop motion devices, yarn storage feeders, and tape drives for knitting machinery.

The Acquisition

In 1968, the company was purchased by Ingersoll-Rand. William Wearly, CEO of Ingersoll-Rand at the time, explained that the acquisition came about almost by accident. He had been impressed with the success of Torrington.

"The ball-bearing industry was a non-growth business. It just moved with the economy. But Torrington, in needle roller bearings, was moving around 8 to 10 percent a year.

When Torrington acquired the C.F. Splitdorf Company in 1912, it gained Splitdorf's ball bearing line, which became the start of a new focus for the business.

They were taking market share and moving up because it was a superior product, technologically speaking.

1945 — Torrington recognized for WWII achievements with Army-Navy "E" Award.

1985 — Fafnir Bearing Division of Textron, Inc. purchased and merged with Torrington.

1994 — Al Nixon becomes president of Torrington.

1968 — Torrington purchased by Ingersoll-Rand.

1992 — J. Frank Travis becomes president of Torrington.

More Leisure and a Cleaner House

Above: Torrington entered the vacuum cleaner business after it purchased the Domestic Sewing Machine Company in 1905.

Right: The Bantam Company, known for its large bearings, was acquired by Torrington in 1901.

"I called the chairman of Torrington and told him this was the age of unfriendly takeovers and we at Ingersoll-Rand were concerned about this, and I thought he at Torrington might be concerned. I said, 'If you're ever involved in an unfriendly takeover, it's good to have some friends. So suppose we become friends.'... I went up to Torrington and spent a day and a half with him. On the second day they brought in their executive vice president, and he said,

'Why don't you come back in a week and tell us what you think we're worth.' ... This absolutely surprised me. I just wanted to be a future white knight.

"I went up to see Torrington the next week and they looked at the offer and said, 'It'll have to be more than that.' And I went back to our treasurer and we came up with a combination of common stock, and we issued a new preferred stock series, which put things over the hill with Torrington. They got this good preferred stock and common stock both. And that did it. They agreed to the deal and within a month we had the deal all signed and sealed."[6]

Wearly later learned that both Bendix and Sperry had been interested in buying Torrington. So Ingersoll-Rand had been a white knight without knowing it. Ingersoll-Rand's 1968 *Annual Report* noted that the merger with Torrington was an example of Ingersoll-Rand's "continuing emphasis on profitably expanding and diversifying ... operations through carefully selected mergers and acquisitions."[7]

After the acquisition, there was very little integration between Torrington and Ingersoll-Rand, noted David C. Garfield, who was liaison between Torrington and Ingersoll-Rand at the time of the acquisition, and president of Ingersoll-Rand from 1981 to 1987. "They wanted to operate pretty much as a stand-alone unit of the company," he recalled. [8]

"I think they were viewed as people who knew how to run their business, so why should we get in and try doing something that was different. It ran pretty much that way and I think there was of course some resentment with Ingersoll-Rand staff people, particularly, who were to a great degree kept apart from Torrington. That of course has essentially gone away, since the staff people have as much insight now into what's going on at Torrington as they do in other units of the company, more or less.

"I think that the people in construction, mining and other units who call themselves Ingersoll-Rand, probably feel a little aloof from Torrington, and they probably feel that the Torrington people are aloof from them and vice versa. So there would be a desire on the part of the Torrington guys to think they have all the opportunities to move into other units and move up the ladder in the company, and perhaps others would like to think they know what's going on in Torrington. I believe this whole situation is more important to the psyche of these guys than it is a practical matter."[9]

Above: Advertisements during World War II reminded those who remained at home how Torrington bearings contributed to the war effort.

Left: Heavy industrial applications, such as this speed reducer of the fifties, employed large spherical roller bearings.

In the past few years, however, a greater effort has been made to integrate the concerns, said J. Frank Travis, president of Torrington from 1992 to 1994.[10]

"Torrington had really been allowed to run totally autonomously for 20 years or so. But the culture of the people was almost identical to the culture of the people that I grew up with at Ingersoll-Rand, which is that they are very dedicated, very hard-working, very dedicated to growing that business.

Left: Torrington expanded its bearing line when it acquired the Fafnir Bearing Division of Textron, Inc. in 1985. At left is the first Fafnir radial bearing, created in 1909.

Below left: During World War II, women filled manufacturing jobs previously held by men, as shown here in Torrington's Bantam division in South Bend, Indiana.

Below right: Allen M. Nixon, president of The Torrington Company since 1994. Nixon was appointed general manager of Torrington's Special Products Division in 1974, and he became vice president and general manager of the Needle Bearings Division in 1983.

"One of the first questions that I asked when I held employee meetings was, 'Why does the door open only into Torrington, rather than out

of Torrington and into Ingersoll-Rand?' And unfortunately, the question was very right-on. I don't think there have been any senior management people that have ever left Torrington and come to another operation of Ingersoll-Rand. Since that time, we've placed a lot of Torrington people within Ingersoll-Rand."[11]

Nixon, who has been president of the division since 1994, said Ingersoll-Rand CEO James Perrella is working to change that perception.

"I'm winding up spending more time at Ingersoll-Rand than I imagined I would have. That's been kind of a surprise. ... We still do our own thing on the business side and the operation side, but the balance between being completely autonomous versus being part of a larger group has worked out very well."[12]

Nixon added that Torrington employees identify more with Torrington than with Ingersoll- Rand. "I do think people are more aware of being part of Ingersoll-Rand than they have been in the past. But the bottom line is, they really identify with their local area, be it a plant in Torrington, Connecticut, or be it The Torrington Company."[13]

After it was acquired, Torrington continued to grow. On October 26, 1985, Ingersoll-Rand purchased the assets of the Fafnir Bearing Division of Textron, Inc., for $103 million in cash, plus the assumption of roughly $60 million in liabilities.[14] Fafnir was merged with Torrington to make Ingersoll-Rand the largest broad-line bearing manufacturer in the United States, and the fifth largest in the world.

The division continues to innovate. In 1987, Torrington introduced bearings with electronic sensors to replace automotive sensing devices which required cables, bulky hardware and extensive wiring. These new bearings were put to use for automatic transmissions and anti-skid

Above: J. Frank Travis, president of Torrington from 1992 to 1994, is now executive vice president of Ingersoll-Rand.

Left: Torrington Nadellager GmbH, in Künsebeck, Germany, produces needle bearings, primarily to international metric standards. The bearings are marketed principally in Germany and Western Europe, with some products exported throughout the world.

braking features that are found in many new cars. The bearings containing electronic sensors have also been found to be useful for electronic steering and advanced differential systems.

"Torrington researchers are also addressing bearing noise, which can interfere with a car's quiet ride. ... To counteract machinery vibration, Torrington has reengineered its manufacturing equipment so that grinding and finishing machinery now produce minimal vibration, and thus, some of the most precise bearings available today. Finally, improved fuel economy, increased reliability and longer life of engine parts are the goals of ongoing research

In 1934, Kendrick's son, Marron, joined the business. In 1946, Walter Schlage died, and his son Ernest continued the family tradition as director of research. In 1953, Charles Kendrick resigned the presidency to become chairman of the board, and Marron Kendrick became president of Schlage.

The company acquired several firms to supplement its offerings in the late fifties and early sixties. "Architects and contractors are prone to group all items of builders' hardware together and ask for a bid on the group," Kendrick explained. "Schlage Lock Company was continuously handicapped in bidding on commercial work, because all of our competitors had door closers and panic exit devices, whereas we had to bid on locks alone. We determined to eliminate this weakness by having a full line of builders' hardware."[21]

In March 1959, Schlage acquired the Peabody Company, which designed luxury hardware, mostly for the main entrance of a building. Peabody became the Schlage Custom Hardware Division. In May 1959, Schlage acquired Louis C. Norton (LCN) Closers, Inc., of Princeton, Illinois, with David Lasier as president.

Above: Schlage expanded its retail program in 1981 to bring quality locks within the reach of do-it-yourself homeowners.

Left: Schlage's push-button lock, patented in 1921, incorporated push-button locking with cylindrical housing, the basic design of the push-button lock used today.

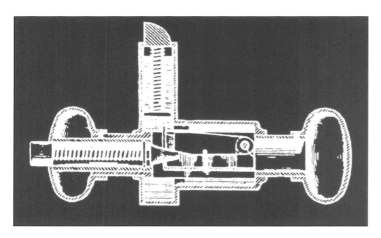

In 1965, Schlage purchased Von Duprin, a company that had been creating panic bars since 1916. Found on the doors of schools and other places, panic bars save lives by easily opening doors in emergency situations, as Lasier explained.

"The impetus behind that was the theater fire in Chicago, where 250 or 280 people died. They

didn't die because they were burned to death. They were trampled in a panic. The exit doors all opened in, and as the people went up against the doors to try and get out, they couldn't open them because of the crush of people behind them. That changed the laws of commercial buildings. Exit doors now must open out."[22]

When Charles Kendrick died in 1970, his son, Marron, became chairman of the board. The family began looking for a company to acquire the business, Lasier said.

A single machine with multiple stations produces Schlage door lock cylinders in 1984.

"It was pretty obvious that if the mother died they would have to sell the Schlage Lock Company to raise money for taxes. Like a lot of companies, they said, 'Let's pick our partner so we don't have to do it under duress at a later date. So Kendrick set out to find a partner that would be compatible, that would be in a similar enough business, but not necessarily in the hardware business, and somebody we could all get along with. We have gotten along with Ingersoll-Rand some 20 years now."[23]

In 1974, Ingersoll-Rand purchased the company in an exchange of stock. "The thing that was not in sync was the product line," noted Dave Garfield, executive vice president at the time, who was Ingersoll-Rand president from 1981 to 1987. "This was overcome by what I might call plain old opportunity. In other words, it became something

that could be done. ... We did it and it worked out wonderfully. It's one of the best elements in the company these days."[24]

Lasier was president of Schlage from 1976 to 1979, when he became president of the entire Door Hardware Group. In 1994, he retired, and Brian D. Jellison became the new president of the group.

"Dave [Lasier] is a big, kind of slow-moving guy," said William Wearly, CEO from 1967 to 1980. "I think the bosses around here all thought of him as going his own direction. Every year, his company just kept going up and up and up. He just did things right. They all said, 'How does he do it? He doesn't seem to do anything, and everything he does works.'"[25]

Ingersoll-Rand also purchased Glynn-Johnson in 1987. Founded in 1926, Glynn-Johnson manufactures door holders, flush bolts, doors stops and other architectural trim.

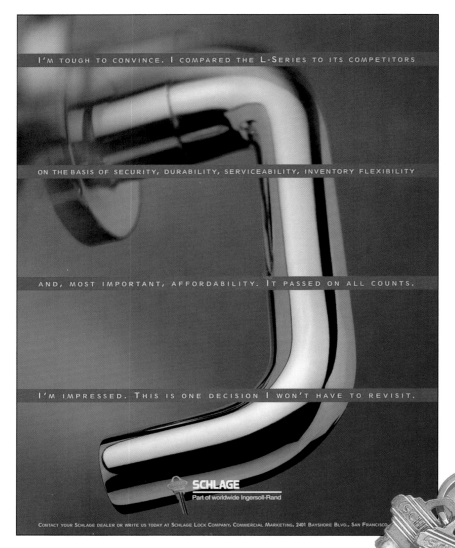

I'M TOUGH TO CONVINCE. I COMPARED THE L-SERIES TO ITS COMPETITORS

ON THE BASIS OF SECURITY, DURABILITY, SERVICEABILITY, INVENTORY FLEXIBILITY

AND, MOST IMPORTANT, AFFORDABILITY. IT PASSED ON ALL COUNTS.

I'M IMPRESSED. THIS IS ONE DECISION I WON'T HAVE TO REVISIT.

SCHLAGE
Part of worldwide Ingersoll-Rand

CONTACT YOUR SCHLAGE DEALER OR WRITE US TODAY AT SCHLAGE LOCK COMPANY, COMMERCIAL MARKETING, 2401 BAYSHORE BLVD., SAN FRANCISCO.

Ingersoll-Rand sold this subsidiary to Westinghouse in 1991. "I think they were not comfortable with the technology and the ability to keep up with the technology," Lasier said. "Ingersoll-Rand is populated by mechanical engineers, not technical engineers."[27]

Today, Schlage, LCN, Von Duprin and Glynn- Johnson comprise Ingersoll-Rand's Door Hardware Group, one of the company's most successful divisions. "For the last 10 or 13 years, the Door Hardware Group has done better than Ingersoll-Rand as a whole," Lasier noted. "It has done quite well in the last five or six years. It has been the top money-maker in the whole corporation."[28]

Innovations have helped the division remain a door industry leader. In 1986, Ingersoll-Rand introduced the KeepSafer from Schlage, a do-it-yourself, wireless home security system. An article in the *Ingersoll-Rand World Report* touted the benefits of the new invention.

"The basic KeepSafer unit consists of a control console and two transmitter/sensor sets, which screw-mount into entry points. When a door or window is opened, contact between the sensors is broken, and an alarm sounds. Several accessories extend KeepSafer's capabilities. These include a glass-break detector; power siren; back-up power supply; medical alarm; and an emergency dialer that contacts police,

The Schlage acquisition included Schlage Electronics Company, formed in 1972, which created electronic security systems, Lasier said.

"It was a computer-based system, multiple doors, using a card access instead of a key. It used a proximity card, so you didn't have to have a key hole. You just leave it in your wallet, and bring it within 6 inches of the target, and it would identify you as somebody who was allowed to pass at this time of day, this day of the week, into that area of the building."[26]

Above left: In 1995, Schlage began a series of four-color advertisements created by advertising agency Suissa-Miller, targeted to architects, locksmiths, building owners, managers and contractors.

fire department or ambulance depending on the emergency.

"Considering the rising crime rate in urban areas, KeepSafer is a welcomed product for single women, as well. Market research indicates that 50 percent of the product's buyers will be female."[29]

The same year, Schlage introduced the Intellis electronic locking system, which revolutionized security in hotels and motels by replacing the traditional room key with a programmed card.

"The system is based on proprietary Macintosh software and a special encoder console. Intellis responds to the hotel industry's need for increased security. Theft prevention, physical safety standards and associated liability increasingly concern hotel managers. The Intellis system allows them to change electronic locking combinations frequently and to program various levels of access onto keycards."[30]

Introduced in 1989, the Maximum Performance Lock could withstand temperature fluctuations from minus 30 degrees to plus 150 degrees, and protect the lock from humidity and airborne contaminants.

In 1991, the Door Hardware Group provided a security package to Comiskey Park, home to the Chicago White Sox.

"Under the contract, Schlage Lock supplied some 900 of its L-9000 series of matrice locks, as well as roughly 1,200 of its new Primus Underwriter Laboratory Cylinder, a high-security patented cylinder. LCN supplied 900 door closers and Von Duprin contributed 300 panic devices, emergency exit devices placed on doors. Glynn-Johnson supplied approximately 65 coordinator bars — used to coordinate the closing of pairs of fire doors, so that they latch shut securely — and a dozen roller latches."[31]

In 1994, a new coating for door hardware provided unprecedented durability. Ingersoll-Rand's Door Hardware Group and the company's Central Material Services Laboratory worked together for five years to develop this new coating, known as ULTIMA. The new ULTIMA coating resists corrosion and is guaranteed by Schlage for 25 years not to tarnish, rust, cloud or discolor. In 1994, Schlage donated 4,000 locks to Habitat for Humanity, the charitable organization that builds affordable housing for those in need.[32] Schlage locks are also used to secure the White House.[33]

A waterjet cutting demonstration in 1985 showed how a specialist cut the glass panels that line the stairway inside the refurbished Statue of Liberty.

CHAPTER ELEVEN

ADDING NEW CAPABILITY

"We have never attempted to diversify outside the general field of machinery and other disciplines involving mechanical engineering. We feel we can be more successful, at less risk to our stockholders, by concentrating our efforts on the field we know."

— William Wearly, 1978

WILLIAM WEARLY and D. Wayne Hallstein set out on an aggressive path of acquisitions when they took the helm of the company in 1967. "Wearly was the growth guy. Everything was growth," said William J. Armstrong, who worked closely with Wearly and is now vice president and treasurer of Ingersoll-Rand.[1] Hallstein recalled that during this acquisition period, he and Wearly "were always insisting that whatever we acquired was going to be number one or number two in its field. And we paid some pretty heavy prices for them."[2]

Waterjet Cutting

Ingersoll-Rand entered the waterjet cutting industry in 1971, and has continuously grown in this market. Waterjet cutting is a revolutionary process that allows manufacturers to repeatedly produce parts with great accuracy. Waterjet cutting systems from Ingersoll-Rand are used worldwide for the production of automobile and aircraft parts, as well as building and insulation materials, the company's annual report explained.

"Waterjet cutting machines are designed to make precision cuts through everything from

candy bars and frozen cake, concrete and even titanium. With computer-controlled robotics, the waterjet can make precision intricate cuts in these and other materials. The waterjet cutter is capable of blasting a stream of water at twice the speed of sound, utilizing fluid pressures up to 60,000 pounds per square inch."[3]

In 1985, the Waterjet Cutting System was used to help prepare the Statue of Liberty for her gala 200th anniversary celebration in New York. The waterjet was used to cut laminated glass panels around the nine-story spiral staircase that leads to her crown, and glass panels in the observation deck of the crown itself.

Acquisitions

The company continued its strategy of acquisition in the seventies. One of the earliest ventures in the seventies was the formation of Ingersoll-

---

Above: Compact, space-saving needle bearings from Ingersoll-Rand's Torrington subsidiary contributed to the rapid development of front-wheel-drive cars.

Rand Pumps Ltd., which purchased the assets of Sigmund Pumps Ltd. This purchase complemented the company's previously acquired pump lines, Cameron and Aldrich.

In 1972, Ingersoll-Rand purchased the Manson Machine Company, which became part of the Lee-Norse Division. Manson manufactured coal-mining machinery such as roof-bolting equipment.

Drilling Accessories and Manufacturing Company (DAMCO) was acquired in 1973, and both the Terry Corporation of Connecticut and the California Pellet Mill Company were acquired in 1974. At the time, the Terry Corporation was a manufacturer of mechanical-drive steam turbines, which complemented other products made by Ingersoll-Rand for the process industry. California Pellet Mill made feed pellets for animals. Perhaps the most important acquisition of the seventies was Ingersoll-Rand's purchase of the Schlage Lock Company in 1974.

New technology led to the use of fiberglass-reinforced polymers to extend pump life in highly corrosive applications.

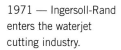

1971 — Ingersoll-Rand enters the waterjet cutting industry.

1972 — Ingersoll-Rand moves from 11 Broadway in New York City to Woodcliff Lake, New Jersey.

1972 — Ingersoll-Rand provides gas turbines for work on a pipeline.

1974 — D. Wayne Hallstein retires and Thomas A. Holmes is made president.

A New Location

In 1972, the company moved its headquarters from 11 Broadway to Woodcliff Lake, New Jersey. The company paid $40,000 an acre for the 85-acre property. "We built on 45 and kept the other 40 as a peach orchard. It was beautiful," Wearly said.[4]

Hallstein, president from 1967 to 1974, recalled that it had become difficult to recruit people because they didn't want to move to New York City.

"New York had an awful reputation. We had almost a 50 percent turnover in clerical personnel, then we had a terrible time trying to promote guys. We couldn't get good guys to come; they wouldn't bring their family into the New York area. You had anywhere from an hour and a half to two hours commuting each way, just to get out to where there's a decent place to live and put your kids in school.

"Johnson and Hopton absolutely refused to move out of the city, so Bill and I, when we were both executive vice presidents, gave up on that because you didn't tell those two guys to do anything.

Above: Ingersoll-Rand world headquarters in Woodcliff Lake, New Jersey.

1974 — Hydraulically-actuated rock drills developed.

1974 — Ingersoll-Rand acquires California Pellet Mill Company.

1974 — Ingersoll-Rand acquires the Terry Corporation of Connecticut.

1977 — Ingersoll-Rand builds the world's fastest rescue drill for the South African Chamber of Mines.

"They were pretty autocratic, and they made all the decisions and approved everything, even the salaries for some of the administrative people. But when I came in, they put me in charge of personnel. We finally got enough of the board members to go along with us to get the hell out of New York and build out at Woodcliff Lake.

"We bought the land and built it, and we didn't get much cooperation from Johnson and Hopton. But when we finally got out there, they admitted it was an improvement. Most of the people went from being an hour and half commuting to 15, 20 minutes. If they lived in Long Island or Westchester or Staten Island, we paid for their move.[5]

Wearly admitted he had been eager to move from New York City.

"We were in an old office building. We kept a beautiful office, but it was a miserable building. The whole part of New York was hard to get to.

"We got out, but I had to be sensitive to the New York people, the people from Long Island that never owned a car. They commuted on the train, on buses, and to move them to New Jersey was very traumatic. ... They had to buy cars and most of them didn't even know how to drive. They had wrecks, but they learned to drive cars."[6]

The Gas Crisis

Ingersoll-Rand responded quickly to the energy crisis of the seventies. When the Organization of Petroleum Exporting Countries (OPEC) embargoed oil to

Niject, a joint venture with Praxair Energy Services, Inc. and the Union Carbide Corporation, built nitrogen plants to provide gaseous nitrogen for reinjection at oil production sites.

nations that had supported Israel in the war against Egypt, domestic gasoline prices skyrocketed and Americans began looking for alternative oil supplies. Ingersoll-Rand executives conducted extensive research and development, looking for the best way to enter this promising market. Eventually, the company decided to form a joint venture with an industrial gas supplier. After more than a year of negotiations, Ingersoll-Rand reached a partnership agreement with Praxair and Union Carbide, Inc., creating Niject Services Company in October 1980. In Niject's first year, it landed profitable contracts with major oil companies such as Getty, Mobil and Amoco. In its first decade, Niject Services earned a reputation as an industry leader.

Even before Niject was formed, the company was involved in finding solutions to the energy shortages. Ingersoll-Rand's mining and drilling tools were widely used for coal mining, which was considered an efficient means to harvest an energy source other than oil. The company's compressors were also critical during the energy crisis, playing an important role in developing pipelines for natural gas and crude oil.

One of the company's most significant projects was its 1972 contract to provide gas turbines for work on a pipeline from the Soviet Union into Austria through Germany, according to Theodore H. Black, CEO from 1988 to 1993. Black, who ran the worldwide sales force at the time, said the contract, worth more than $10 million, was the largest to date for Ingersoll-Rand. But it was controversial. "That was very unpopular around the world because there was a question of the economic dependence of Europe on Soviet energy and whether it was worth the price."[7]

In 1973, Ingersoll-Rand introduced the Centregal, a high-pressure centrifugal compressor. This model was useful for natural gas conservation and gas-gathering work. This model was also designed with a space-saving housing, which made it easier to maintain.

Centrifugal air compressors at DuPont's Seaford, Delaware, nylon-fiber manufacturing plant are operated by Niject Services Company, Ingersoll-Rand's Enhanced Oil Recovery Company.

In 1974, Ingersoll-Rand introduced the world's largest downhole air power drill, used extensively during construction of the trans-Alaskan pipeline, which was completed in 1977.

Also in the seventies, the company established Ingersoll-Rand Compression Services to lease compressors on a contract basis. Known as the Big Red Fleet, these mobile compressors would harness gas and oil from wells that had been capped or considered depleted.

Keeping Track of a Growing Company

To handle the company's continued growth, Thomas McBride was hired as corporate controller in 1974. "It was a real challenge," McBride said.

"Frankly, from the financial life cycle of a business, it was pretty far behind. The company was very strong in its marketing, sales,

duced a 30-inch-diameter downhole Superdrill for the South African Chamber of Mines. The Superdrill was described in the 1977 *Annual Report* as a machine that could revolutionize mine rescue work. On June 8, 1991, the Superdrill lived up to this reputation when it saved the lives of 26 trapped mine workers after the roof collapsed in the Emaswati coal mine in Swaziland. The dramatic rescue was described in *Ingersoll-Rand World Report*.

> *"The Superdrill reached the mine and at 3:15 the morning after the accident, began work. With its thundering hammerdrill pounding away, it bored a 25-inch hole through approximately 215 feet of earth, coal and debris in the direction of the trapped men. Eight and one-half hours after it began its task, the drill broke through. The miners were lifted to safety by means of a steel capsule, manned by a team of specially trained brigadesmen. ... The largest downhole drill in the world, the Superdrill was designed with emergencies such as Emaswati in mind. ... Prior to the development of the Superdrill, the best the Emaswati miners could have hoped for was a three- week, around-the-clock rescue mission."[13]*

Ingersoll-Rand provided drilling equipment for major projects around the world. In 1977 alone, Ingersoll-Rand equipment was put to work on California Interstate 15, the James Bay, Quebec, hydroelectric project, excavation at Brazil's Itaipu Dam, and the drilling of thousands of water wells for both commercial and residential purposes. New drills in 1978 included a blast-hole unit and a truck-mounted Drillmaster designed for use by the water well industry.

Developments in Compressors

Compressors from Ingersoll-Rand began to see increasingly diversified applications in the seventies. High-pressure compressors, such as

Ingersoll-Rand drilling rigs are used to find water in traditionally arid regions. This 1975 photograph shows an Ingersoll-Rand water well drill tapping an underground water source in the Middle East.

Ingersoll-Rand's Superdrill series of downhole drills is used in applications that require drilling large-diameter holes in rock. Here, workers at the massive Hitokura Dam project in Japan use a 24-inch-diameter drill before stabilizing the soft sandstone and clay slate of a broad mountainside.

the Super Slugger, were used in the plastics industry to manufacture polyethylene, a raw material needed for products such as sandwich bags and food wrappers.

In 1974, the company introduced two new lines of nonlubricated oil-free reciprocating compressors. In 1975, a line of multi-stage centrifugal compressors that delivered improved efficiency rates, a line of packaged air compressors for construction, and a silenced high-pressure portable compressor were all introduced.

By 1979, Ingersoll-Rand was able to state in the annual report that its Air Compressor Group had record sales and the most complete line of compressors in the industry.

More Acquisitions, and a Divestiture

Other acquisitions in the second half of the seventies included Cyclone Drill in 1975; Sier Bath Gear Company, a manufacturer of gears and couplings, in 1976; S&S Corporation, a

This large-scale gold-mining operation uses Ingersoll-Rand truck-mounted rotary drills for cost-effective productivity.

manufacturer of underground mine haulage equipment, in 1976; and Western Land Roller, an irrigation equipment manufacturer, in 1977.

During this impressive period of acquisition, the company divested its Condenser Division in January 1977. This division had been involved with condensers since 1916, when a Condenser and Pump department was established to sell barometric condensers designed by Herman Beyer. By 1920, the company had begun working with surface condensers. While barometric condensers are applied for the evaporation of solutions, surface condensers are designed to save the collected condensation. During the time that Ingersoll-Rand was involved in the condenser industry, its condensers were widely used in power plants. According to the 1976 *Annual Report*, the sale of the Condenser Division was not expected to "have any material impact on the company's financial statements."[14]

In a 1978 speech to the Stockbrokers Society, Wearly reflected on the company's growth strategy.

"We have diversified our company greatly over the past few years, and I would like to dwell on this philosophy for a moment.

"First, we have never attempted to diversify outside the general field of machinery and other disciplines involving mechanical engineering. We feel we can be more successful, at less risk to our stockholders, by concentrating our efforts on the field we know.

"Second, in most of our lines we are either the number one or number two company. This is a conscious effort on our part. ... When we are not able to obtain the first or second market share position in a given area, we will normally close up our operations and direct our attention to more profitable businesses.

"The third factor, which I think is important to understand about Ingersoll-Rand Company, relates to the word 'diversified.' We are not diversified in our general approach to business, since we have stayed in the machinery and allied products industry emphasizing mechanical engineering. We are diversified, however, in terms of the different kinds of machinery we make and the markets to which we sell that machinery."[15]

Large blasthole drills, such as this rig operating at a mine in Scranton, Pennsylvania, are at work on six continents to help nations develop critical energy resources.

CHAPTER TWELVE

NEW ALLIANCES

*"While many American manufacturers talk about joint ventures,
Ingersoll had learned to carry them out, and carry them out well."*

—*Barron's*

THOMAS A. HOLMES was elected chairman of the board and CEO on January 1, 1981, replacing William Wearly, who had held the post since 1967. After graduating from the Missouri School of Mines with a degree in mining engineering in 1950, Holmes began his career with Ingersoll-Rand as a trainee, moving up through sales and management positions. He became the general manager of the Rock Drill Division in 1964, and three years later was appointed general manager of the Construction and Mining Group. In 1968, Holmes became a vice president, and a year later he was elected as an executive vice president. He continued his education, earning a law degree from Lafayette College in 1981, and graduated from the Harvard Business School Advanced Management Program.

In 1981, David C. Garfield became president of Ingersoll-Rand. Garfield joined the company in 1952, and was the company's representative in Japan from 1953 to 1959. He became vice president of the company in 1964, and served on the board of directors from 1964 to 1985. He was elected vice chairman in 1974.

Growth in the Eighties

Ingersoll-Rand began the eighties with a continuation of the aggressive growth campaign that it had followed since the sixties. In 1980, the company purchased the Machinery Division of Cabot Corporation, which manufactured mobile drilling equipment, service and workover rigs for the oil and gas industry, as well as Knight Industries, an assembling and packaging concern that joined the Gas Compressor Group.

In 1980, the line of downhole drills was expanded to include a new hydraulically powered crawler drill. Ingersoll-Rand drill rigs were enjoying increasing popularity in developing nations, where they were being used on important infrastructure projects. In 1981, for example, Ingersoll-Rand drills were used to put in water wells in Somalia, where drought and famine were ravaging the population. In 1987, water well construction was expanded to India and Ghana.

The Air Compressor Group introduced high performance centrifugal air compressors with expanded capacity and pressure ranges. In 1981, Ingersoll-Rand entered the snow-making market, supplying multiple-packaged, high-capacity rotary air compressors to many ski resorts. Even when company sales declined in 1982, this market segment performed well.

Resorts around the world extend their skiing seasons with the help of air compressors from Ingersoll-Rand.

Folley had been hired from Price Waterhouse in 1981, where he had handled Ingersoll-Rand's account for many years. The company needed to take drastic measures to recover, McBride said.

"We were faced with a significant problem, and this company had never had a serious lay-off situation before. One of the prides of the company was that it was fairly paternalistic. But the company's choice was, 'Do you want to save 31,000 jobs or do you want to lose all 49,000 of them?' We had a couple of big meetings, and we came up with a restructuring plan. We put a game plan together that was pretty cohesive and pretty broad-based. I give Holmes a lot of credit. We got rid of almost a third of the company. Once you got over the emotional aspect, it was pretty clear it had to be done."[2]

"He had a tough job, reducing those people," said William Wearly, CEO from 1967 to 1980. He noted that in 1980, Ingersoll-Rand had about 54,000 employees and generated about a billion dollars annually in sales. In 1995, the company has about 34,000 people and generates $4.5 billion in sales.

"Ingersoll-Rand did this before many other companies did it. Tom Holmes started doing this tough job of cutting out people, and that was a tough job for anyone to do. I'm glad he did it because I might not have been as good at it."[3]

An offshore platform in the North Sea represented an excellent market for pumps, compressors, hoists and tools, but a market that decreased significantly in the early 1980s, creating problems for then-Chairman Thomas Holmes.

Some of the less profitable businesses were sold. In August 1984, Ingersoll-Rand sold its Proto industrial hand tool division and its cutting tool product line to The Stanley Works for $43 million in cash. A line of knitting needles was also sold. Throughout the world, manufacturing plants were closed. "My job in 1983 was closing operations, as much as anything," said J. Frank Travis, president of the European Served Area at the time.[4]

Management functions and sales offices were consolidated. The company also sold 40 acres of prime real estate in Woodcliff Lake, New Jersey, to BMW. This sale represented approximately half of the land that Ingersoll-Rand had purchased to build its new headquarters in 1971. BMW paid $500,000 per acre on land that Ingersoll-Rand had acquired for $40,000 an acre, Wearly said. "BMW paid $20 million dollars, which was more than we had paid for the whole place," he said. "But that's what happened to real estate."[5]

Director Alexander Massad, retired executive vice president of Mobil Oil, who was on the board while Holmes was chairman, said Holmes was working under difficult circumstances. "I think [Holmes] was in an unusual situation in which the earnings were impacted severely, and he had to pull in his horns a little bit," he said.[6]

In addition to cutting costs, Ingersoll-Rand looked for new ways to generate profit. Holmes believed that growth in the auto industry would benefit Ingersoll-Rand, since the company produces bearings that are essential in front-wheel-drive vehicles.

A crawler drill, with its onboard air compressor, has enhanced maneuverability which simplifies operations.

Even during this difficult time, Ingersoll-Rand made some small acquisitions and formed a few joint ventures. In 1983, Ingersoll-Rand acquired various operating assets of Porta Drill, Inc., expanding the line of portable drills that Ingersoll-Rand sold to the water well market. In late 1983 and early 1984, the company formed an agreement with the German turbine manufacturer, AEG-Kanis and Al-Jon, Inc., for hydrostatically driven landfill compactors.

But companies such as Atlas Copco, a Swedish firm, were aggressively competing with Ingersoll-Rand's compressor lines. An article in *Financial World* noted that Holmes' recovery plan seemed ambitious.

"*Holmes, though unwilling to spell out a specific revival program, has articulated a number of pretty lofty financial goals. He wants to lift sales 10 percent to 12 percent annually over the next five years. That may be attainable. But three other goals will prove more challenging. Holmes wants after-tax margins to rise to 7.5 percent, a return the company hasn't achieved since 1973. He also wants to push his return on assets up to 10 percent and return on equity to 18 percent, two returns no one ever remembers the company earning.*"[7]

His plan may have been ambitious, but Holmes led Ingersoll-Rand back to prosperity. By

The largest steam turbine ever produced by the Wellsville, New York, facility bears the nameplate of Dresser-Rand, an Ingersoll-Rand joint venture.

equal partnership joint venture designed to handle the worldwide reciprocating compressor and turbo machinery products of both firms. "That has been *extremely* successful," said Theodore Black, who was in charge of mergers and acquisitions at the time and became CEO of the newly formed concern.[12]

Black recalled that the two companies were familiar with each other because their big compressors were in competition with each other. At the time, the energy business was not doing well and the drilling rate count dropped substantially, Black said.

"The market was really shrinking. All the businesses were somewhat impaired. We were losing money. Dresser was marginally making some money. Dresser was very good in this turbo machinery business. We were very good in the reciprocating gas business, we had the premier position."[13]

Though it is uncertain which organization first formally proposed the union, the idea wasn't totally unexpected, Black suggested.

"At these industry meetings, you're standing around, having a drink, and you say, 'Maybe some day we ought to put these businesses together and create something that's really big and complementary.' The turndown in the market gave the impetus to do this. If you're not making money, or you're making a lot less money than you should be making, it gets your attention."[14]

The joint venture was scrutinized by the federal government much the way an acquisition is examined, to make sure it does not violate antitrust regulations. Since both businesses were not performing well, the process was easier than usual, Black said.

"We didn't do it because we thought it would float through the Justice Department or the Commerce Department. We did it because it was the right thing to do. Coincidentally, they would see that this business was not making any money. ... Actually, the market has impaired businesses, that's the phrase that's used in Washington, which means it could go out of business, and there would be one less competitor anyway."[15]

The 50-50 joint venture was approved in 1986. Black had carefully worked out the specifics of the deal, including which plants would close. More than 1,000 people were laid off, for a savings of $44 million. "In each case, we had two of everything." Black said. "We had two big turbo machinery plants here, two in Europe, et cetera. Two managers. ... A 50-50 joint venture is considered next to impossible, because one guy gets greedy or selfish or the culture is different. This worked like a charm."[16]

The effectiveness of the joint venture was remarkable, given the scale of the project. The press agreed, as indicated by this praise from *Barron's* magazine.

"While many American manufacturers talk about joint ventures, Ingersoll had learned to carry them out, and carry them out well. One of the most notable came in 1986. Ted Black, during his climb through the company ranks, had long been a friendly rival of top people at Dresser Industries, another major supplier of products and technical service for oil and gas exploration and production. Over the odd golf game and hunting trip, Black and Jack Murphy, now Dresser's chairman and chief executive, found that they both had similar problems with their struggling energy opera-

tions. They came up with a plan to merge the operations into a joint venture, Dresser-Rand.

"Operations began the first day of 1987 with involvement from several divisions of Ingersoll-Rand, including the Terry Steam Turbine, Turbo Machinery, Engine Process Compressor, Compression Services and part of the Engineered Equipment Repair Division.

"Black was made CEO of the billion-dollar venture, a job that he considered good training for his eventual rise to CEO of Ingersoll-Rand. He noted that the venture was held at a dis-

Employees at Dresser-Rand's Houston facility inspect machinery manufactured to help Venezuela boost oil production in 1991. Dresser-Rand, a joint venture between Dresser Industries and Ingersoll-Rand, produces equipment for the energy industry.

An Ingersoll-Rand technician in Vignate, Italy, examines a large centrifugal compressor prior to final assembly. The company's centrifugal air compressor line was expanded in 1984 to include a large capacity unit suited for major processing industries.

tance from both Ingersoll and Dresser. 'We wanted to prove we were at arms length. I didn't belong to Dresser, I didn't belong to Ingersoll-Rand. We emphasized that. I think that's one of the reasons it worked.'"[17]

New Compressors for a Changing Market

In 1984, the company introduced a line of energy-efficient small compressors. The new product line included both the ChargeAir Pro and EnergAir machines, designed for low horsepower use. "The energy efficiency of the compressor is more and more important around the world," said Steve Doolittle, general manager of GHH-RAND Schraubenkompressoren GmbH &

Company in Oberhausen, Germany. "It's always been important in Europe and now it's becoming more important in America."[18]

The centrifugal air compressor line was expanded in 1984 to include a large capacity unit suited for major processing industries. This model was the largest integral gear air compressor that Ingersoll-Rand had ever built up to that point. The centrifugal line was not only expanded to include larger units, but smaller ones as well. One new model, developed in Europe, was designed to fit the demand for a nonlubricated air compressor rated below 1,000 cubic feet per minute.

Among new products in 1985, Ingersoll-Rand introduced a low-pressure dynamic compressor known as the X-Flo. Also in 1985, a ChargeAir Pro Workshop Series was developed for use in homes and small shops. Ingersoll-Rand's rotary air compressors were redesigned to be more efficient and economical, as well as easier to manufacture. New gas compressors included a unit designed to handle many types of gases while being reliable under even the most extreme working conditions. A special portable compressor was designed with the United States Army in mind, equipped with rugged air tools and able to withstand difficult battlefield conditions.

The X-Flo single-stage turbo compressors, which included some compact units, were introduced in 1986. The same year, Sweden ordered a large number of portable air compressors to be used by its civil defense operations in the event of military emergencies.

The financial markets around the world fluctuated drastically as the stock market plunged in 1987, and the dollar value was unsteady in foreign markets. The compressor lines, however, experienced continued success. New lower-capacity models were added to the centrifugal compressor line, as were steam compressors for use in the chemical process industry. New ChargeAir Pro products included the Air Bench, model WB-700, a combination workbench and storage chest specially designed for air-powered equipment, and a spray cleaner accessory for cleaning, disinfecting and degreasing applications.[19]

In 1988, for the first time, Ingersoll-Rand rotary air compressors were used in facilities in which energy was produced from garbage while reducing noxious emissions to meet acceptable environmental levels.

Drills for Energy and the Environment

In the eighties, specialized Ingersoll-Rand drills were designed with environmental considerations in mind. In 1984, a small drill rig was introduced for well drilling and mineral exploration. According to the 1984 *Annual Report*, these rigs could determine if potentially hazardous materials had seeped from landfills.

The market for surface drills also expanded, with successful marketing of the largest blasthole drill ever made by Ingersoll-Rand. These drills

Three Ingersoll-Rand pumps, installed on the support rings shown above, can move more than 1 million gallons of water per minute out of the Great Salt Lake to alleviate flooding.

were first used in China in 1985 to open new coal mines, an important energy source for China's burgeoning population.

The Strike Force 6 downhole hammer drill, introduced in 1986, dramatically increased drilling rates. Also in 1986, the Rotary Drill Division introduced the DM-M Drillmaster, a crawler mounted, multipass rotary drilling rig, capable of drilling 9- to 10-inch blast-holes. This new Drillmaster, targeted toward the coal industry, was one of many products that Ingersoll-Rand displayed at the 1986 American Mining Congress show in Las Vegas.

In 1987, Ingersoll-Rand products helped prevent flooding at the Great Salt Lake in Utah. Water levels had been rising continually since 1982, and Ingersoll-Rand was able to provide vertical flood control pumps powered by natural gas engines. The result was a reduction in the water level by almost 4 feet.

Other Acquisitions

In 1987, Ingersoll-Rand made several relatively small acquisitions. The company acquired Beebe International, Inc., a Seattle-based firm that produced winches for industrial and marine applications. California Pellet Mill Company, a subsidiary of Ingersoll-Rand, acquired Iowa-based Roskamp Manufacturing, which produced rolling and flaking mills for grain processing. Two other small acquisitions in 1987 were Glynn-Johnson, a specialty door controls manufacturing company from Chicago, and specific assets involving commercial bearings of the New Departure-Hyatt Division of General Motors.

Growing Opportunities in China

In 1987, Ingersoll-Rand forged two joint ventures in China and established Ingersoll-Rand China Limited (IRCL). The first joint venture with Xuanhua Pneumatic Machinery Factory of Hebei Province formed Xuanhua Ingersoll-Rand Mining and Construction Machinery Limited (XHIR), a 50-50 joint venture involved in the manufacture of drills. The second joint venture was with Shanghai Compressor Factory to create Shanghai Ingersoll-Rand Compressor Limited (SIRC), which manufactures portable compressors and several models of stationary compressors. Daniel Kletter, vice president in charge of China operations, organized construction of the compressor plant. "We went to a green field site, built a whole new plant, a pretty interesting plant by China's standards. We used the same technology we use in our U.S. facilities, and it's been very successful."[20]

Today, SIRC employs about 200 people and is expecting $16 million in sales in 1995, Kletter said. "We're sort of the heart of what the Chinese are buying today, and we're expanding in that range."[21]

Left: Chinese executives presented Chairman Thomas A. Holmes with a commemorative album covering the signing of the partnership contract in 1987.

"The business conditions in China are unique. You're dealing with a combination of local customers and multinational companies. The reason we got in there was they had the capacity to sell in local currency. It was becoming more difficult to import products and these kinds of equipment. We found early on that we had to get paid up front for the product because receivables were very difficult to collect given the triangular debt, in which one company owes another company, which owes another company.

"There were a number of unique things that we had to work our way through. Issues with the government had to be resolved, as well as getting approval for the building we wanted to build and dealing with local suppliers and bringing them up to the quality we needed, and dealing with the various ministries, and then philosophically dealing with the partner who had never really had to run a business. Orders were always given to them by the central government, and they always worked according to that schedule. So we had to do a lot of training. We had to train their people in the American ways of doing business."[22]

Western-style houses were built for the general manager and technical specialist, Kletter said, because "the Chinese tend to live in massive apartment buildings."[23]

CEO James Perrella said joint ventures in China are beneficial to both parties. "These joint ventures are there because we needed somebody who knew the territory. The other thing was, they weren't going to let us in alone anyway. To get in, we had to have a partner. ... That's why joint ventures makes sense in China."[24]

New Marketing Strategies

In 1986, the Air Compressor Group of Ingersoll-Rand began a telemarketing campaign that included follow-up calls to compressor customers. An article in *Ingersoll-Rand World Report* extolled the success of the program.

"The telemarketing program has been so successful that it has brought in $1.2 million in maintenance, parts and service revenue, as well as $1.6 million in outstanding quotes. It has also increased goodwill and improved customer relations. ... After consolidating the database, the telemarketers have identified the owners and locations of more than 12,000 Ingersoll-Rand compressors. This allows the company to give the owners the individualized attention they needed."[25]

In 1987, the company began an air compressor marketing program targeted toward distributors. Called "Road America," the program involved putting centrifugal air compressors on trucks and driving them to distributors around the United States for demonstrations. The same year, portable air compressors from the Mocksville, North Carolina plant were affixed with decals that read, "Employee Involvement teams at work." These teams made significant improvements in production that greatly boosted efficiency.

INGERSOLL ROCK DRILLS have been used in China since before the turn of the century. Before World War II, Ingersoll-Rand contributed materials that were critical to the development of China's infrastructure. In the past 15 years, trade relations between the United States and China have improved. In 1984, the company opened a branch in Beijing. Ingersoll-Rand China, established in 1987, participates in two joint ventures — Xuanhua Ingersoll-

China

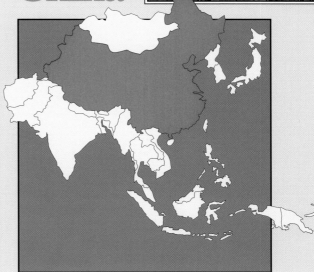

Rand Mining and Construction Machinery Ltd., and Shanghai Ingersoll-Rand Compressor, Ltd. In 1993, the CPM-Zhengchang Liyang Machinery Machinery Company Limited joint venture was formed to assemble and market pellet mills and manufacture dies and other related products.

Shaping a new horizon along the Santiago River for the Aquamilpa hydroelectric project are Ingersoll-Rand crawler drills used in the excavation of the dam's diversion works and surge chambers. The project will expand Mexico's horizons by generating more than 2,100 million kilowatt hours of power per year. In all, 25 Ingersoll-Rand drills and a like number of portable air compressors were involved.

CHAPTER THIRTEEN

NEW HORIZONS

"'We are not a glamorous company,' says Ingersoll-Rand Company Chairman Theodore Black, between puffs on his unfiltered Camel cigarette. 'But what's glamour compared with profitability?'"

— *Forbes*, 1993.

THE TOTAL QUALITY Leadership concept, adopted in late 1987, is a company-wide initiative to improve the quality of the entire business, from the customer order, to manufacturing, to delivery and installation, to service. CEO James Perrella noted that the Total Quality Leadership program sprang from the grass roots of the company.

"Each of the divisions and groups themselves decided to tackle some form of Total Quality Management. They didn't all call it Total Quality Management. All we did at the corporate level was support the efforts of the individuals taking the challenge. We said they had to establish some quality goals, and they all did their own thing. Some divisions stayed with it, others didn't. What we did at the corporate level was provide a communication and a coordination in bringing out the best that was being accomplished."[1]

James Lahey, director of Total Quality Leadership, likes to tell a story that typifies how Ingersoll-Rand has changed since the Total Quality Program.

"During my first week on the job as a welder in 1977, I had a really good idea. I went to my supervisor, Bob, and said, 'I was up last night and I had an idea of how we can change the angle of the blade we're welding and reduce the outflow and reduce grinding.' He stopped me halfway through and said, 'Jim, there's something very important you have to understand. We pay you to weld, not to think.' So I went back to the job. A couple of weeks later, the idea came out of the front office, and of course, Bob went in and talked to somebody, and all of a sudden he had a great idea. That's the way Ingersoll-Rand was prior to the eighties."[2]

Lahey also heads the Total Quality Leadership Council, which consists of group executives.

"We get together on a regular basis to look at what we're doing in this organization and outside this organization. We have had the Vice president of Quality from Westinghouse come in and talk to our council. As a group, we have taken them to Ford Motor Company. Jim Perrella [chairman and CEO] came along on that trip. We took them to Motorola.

Above: Ingersoll-Rand's global culture is symbolized as a hard-hat, generated by the company for a road-building awareness campaign.

"There are a couple of things that you really have to focus on in an organization, and this comes directly from Motorola. One is customer satisfaction, one is cycle time reduction, and one is defect reduction. Motorola has a process where, once you baseline where you are in customer satisfaction, cycle time reduction or defect reduction, you're required to improve that by about 66 percent over each year. That becomes your new baseline, and you improve that 66 percent. When we saw that, we liked it. But Barry Uber, who really was the first to adopt it here, said, 'That's too much math.' And he went with 50 percent.

"The interesting thing is that you can never get there. Basically, it's a systematic way that Motorola looks at improvement. It really is a matter of leadership, setting goals, then putting people to work that understand the process, to really use the tools we have been teaching over the years. Those are admirable goals because they are all tied together. Customer satisfaction is impacted by quality defects and by cycle time. You have to reduce defects to improve cycle time, and if you do

both those things, you'll have lower overhead costs, which can be fed back to the customer in lower price, or delivered to the stockholder as increased dividends."[3]

In 1994, Total Quality posters at the headquarters in Woodcliff Lake, New Jersey, displayed an inspiring quote from Perrella.

"We must motivate customers to choose Ingersoll-Rand. We must perform our assignments so well, make our products to such high standards of quality, that it would be difficult to choose another company's products or services." [4]

Top Prices for Top Quality

Perrella noted that Ingersoll-Rand products have traditionally commanded top prices in the field.

"There's no question that we have had premium prices. We have had the best people in the field to service our customers, so it wasn't just our superior product. It was the product and the people. We have more competition today. You

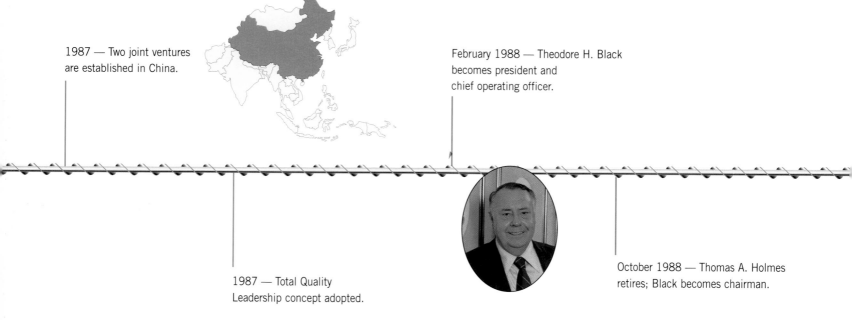

1987 — Two joint ventures are established in China.

February 1988 — Theodore H. Black becomes president and chief operating officer.

1987 — Total Quality Leadership concept adopted.

October 1988 — Thomas A. Holmes retires; Black becomes chairman.

can't maintain the top-quality best position very long without being challenged, so you have to keep moving to the next level."[5]

Retired salesman Stan Orben, who was hired in 1929, agreed. "Even today, Ingersoll-Rand is respected because it has a quality image created over the past one hundred years," he said.

"Thousands of Ingersoll-Rand people, including designers, draftsmen, service personnel and secretaries contributed to that image. It took a hell of a long while to build up. The company now has a quality image, and a customer is certainly aware that quality has a price tag on it."[6]

Theodore H. Black

Theodore H. Black assumed his duties as president and chief operating officer in February 1988, and was elected to the board. By October of that year, Black had become the next chairman of the board, while Holmes retired after 38 years with Ingersoll-Rand.

Left to right: Theodore H. Black, Thomas A. Holmes, Clyde H. Folley.

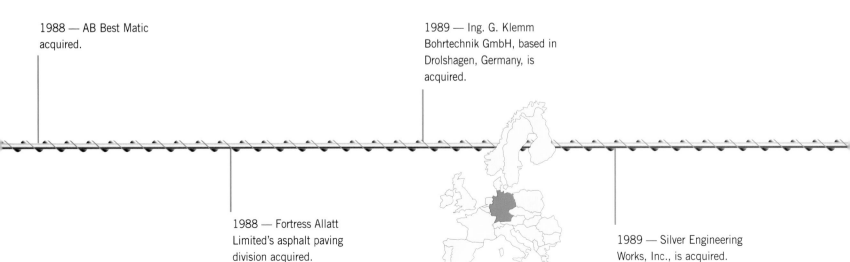

1988 — AB Best Matic acquired.

1989 — Ing. G. Klemm Bohrtechnik GmbH, based in Drolshagen, Germany, is acquired.

1988 — Fortress Allatt Limited's asphalt paving division acquired.

1989 — Silver Engineering Works, Inc., is acquired.

Theodore H. Black was president of Ingersoll-Rand from 1988 to 1992, and chairman of the board from 1988 to 1993. Black began his career with Ingersoll-Rand in 1957. In 1993, net sales reached the $4 billion level for the first time in Ingersoll-Rand history. In the 1993 *Annual Report*, James E. Perrella, the current chairman, president and CEO, saluted the work accomplished by Black. "Under Ted's leadership, our company achieved its highest annual earnings in 1989. Most impressive, however, was Ingersoll-Rand's stalwart performance during the extended recession that gripped the United States and Europe at various points from 1990 through 1993. We are fortunate that we retain Ted's expertise as a member of our board of directors."

Black graduated from the U.S. Naval Academy in 1953 with an engineering degree, and began working for Ingersoll-Rand in 1957 as an application engineer. In 1972, he became a vice president, and in 1982, he became president of the Pump and Turbo Machinery groups. In 1983, he was named vice president of Mergers and Acquisitions.

When Dresser-Rand was formed in 1986, Black became president and CEO of the joint venture.

Black maintained a conservative perspective about Ingersoll-Rand during his time as chairman, as a 1993 *Forbes* article noted.

> "'We are not a glamorous company,' says Ingersoll-Rand Company Chairman Theodore Black, between puffs on his unfiltered Camel cigarette. 'But what's glamour compared with profitability?' In Forbes' Annual Report on American Industry (Jan. 4), Ingersoll-Rand was by far the most profitable of the large heavy-equipment makers. A maker of machinery and parts for the auto, construction and industrial equipment industries, Ingersoll-Rand scarcely noticed the recession."[7]

Black admitted that his biggest challenge was to continue the cost reductions and product improvements that had been initiated by Thomas Holmes and William Wearly. "We eventually wound up with some record earnings during my period of time. We made some pretty good acquisitions. Not all great, but good."[8]

In 1993, Black was named winner of the gold award in the machinery industry by the *Wall Street Transcript*, a publication that recognizes CEOs in various industries based on reports by financial analysts. The same year, *Financial World* named Black CEO of the Year in the category of industrial equipment. The award recognizes achievement among chief executive officers of public companies with at least $100 million in revenues or assets.[9]

Germany

In 1989, Ingersoll-Rand acquired Ing. G. Klemm Bohrtechnik GmbH of Drolshagen, a West German manufacturer of special-purpose hydraulic rock drills and related equipment. This acquisition enhanced Ingersoll-Rand's ability to serve the civil engineering market.

In 1994, Germany began to clean up landfill sites that had been used as dump sites a century ago, and the country relied on Klemm's new jet grouting drill, designed to protect the environment by sealing hazardous waste sites.

Ingersoll–Rand's worldwide experience in providing machines and equipment for big construction projects, including roads and tunnels, led to the selection of the company's air compressors to power tools and hoists during construction of the historic English Channel Tunnel.

"One of the leaders in providing it is Ing G. Klemm Bohrtechnik GmbH (Klemm), a unit of worldwide Ingersoll-Rand. Klemm provides environmental drilling products that make it possible to isolate and contain landfilled toxic wastes. ... Using Klemm products, workers carefully drill vertical holes and horizontal basement holes in the affected areas. Then, chemical resins, grout and bentonite (a clay material that absorbs liquids readily) are injected into the holes to seal them and prevent the chemicals from migrating. A popular tool for this job is the Klemm KR806 drill, a 109kW (147hp) unit powering a double-head system. In this system, one head powers the casing that protects the hole from collapsing; the other head does the actual drilling."[10]

Building Roads

With good roads, food and products are delivered to markets. People can get to work. Cities are linked to the countryside. In developng nations, roads can make the difference between poverty and prosperity. Ingersoll-Rand's road-building efforts have enhanced the economic and social progress in virtually every country in the world.

In 1988, Ingersoll-Rand's Construction Equipment Group acquired Fortress Allatt Limited's asphalt paving equipment division, marking its entry into the asphalt paving business. "We now had a milling machine (to remove old surface); a paving machine (to apply the new surface); and a vibratory compactor (to compact it and make the road surface ready to use)."[11]

In 1988, the Compaction Division changed its name to the Road Machinery Division. Through the $35.4 million acquisition of ABG Verwaltungs GmbH and related entities in 1990, Ingersoll-Rand continued this program to expand its line of paving equipment and road machinery.

Paving equipment from Ingersoll-Rand has been used worldwide. One project involving ABG pavers was at the Jing-Jin-Tang expressway in China in the early 1990s. This road connects Beijing, the capital, and Tianjin, China's largest seaport to the north. Another major highway project in the early 1990s, the M8 Motorway in Scotland, which marked the sale of the first ProCut 2200 milling machine. Also used in the refurbishing was an Ingersoll-Rand MT-7000 milling machine, and Ingersoll-Rand HP750 air compressors.

Other Acquisitions

In 1988, Ingersoll-Rand acquired AB Best Matic, a Swedish designer of Waterjet cutting systems. In 1989, Ingersoll-Rand expanded its Improved Paper Machinery Corporation (IMPCO) Division when it acquired Silver Engineering Works, Inc., which supplied machinery to many industries, including the pulp and paper industries.

Above: An asphalt compactor operating on Interstate 40 near Barstow, California. Ingersoll-Rand's diverse line of road-building and repair machinery continues to expand.

Right: Runways at Tokyo's Narita International Airport were prepared for resurfacing in 1987 by one of Ingersoll-Rand's large pavement milling machines.

Above: DM-M rotary drill at Kansai International Airport, Osaka.

Right: Ingersoll-Rand crawler drill at Hibernia Oil platform, Canada.

Pressure Systems, Inc., manufacturer of Eagle Air Systems since 1972, was also acquired in 1989, bringing Ingersoll-Rand into a market that sold breathing systems to fire fighters, emergency rescue, sports, professional and military diving, and industrial sandblasting and painting. Ingersoll-Rand also acquired the batch centrifuge business of Nils Weibull AB, and the hammermill business of Champion products in 1989.

Building Throughout the World

In 1989, Ingersoll-Rand's subsidiary, Torrington, provided the largest spherical roller bearings ever made, designed for the reconstruction of the Burlington-Northern Bridge, which passes over the Williamette River in Portland, Oregon.

The Bonneville Dam lock on the Columbia River near Portland was causing a traffic jam of boats waiting to pass through. The United States Army Corps of Engineers undertook the project of constructing a new lock at the dam. This project was constructed with the use of Ingersoll-Rand equipment, including light towers, compressors, rough-terrain fork lifts, superdrills, pavement breakers, air tools and downhole drills, according to *Ingersoll-Rand World Report*.

"In discussing Ingersoll-Rand's success in placing the lion's share of equipment on the project, equipment salesman Jeff Heineman said, 'Our success in the Bonneville Dam project is the result of a big team effort between the Portland and Seattle equipment sales offices. We had a lot of pressure from the competition, especially in the ground engineering area, but we were able to capitalize on Ingersoll-Rand's reputation for great service and high-quality products.' A focal point of the project for the Corps has been two Ingersoll-Rand KR 806D Klemm drills. Outfitted with double-head drilling systems and DHD-350 downhole drills, the Klemm drills used a lost-crown system to complete two to three, 160-foot-deep holes per day in extremely difficult drilling conditions, including unconsolidated material, full of boulders, loose gravel, sand and clay."[12]

A Reputation for Quality

International demands for drills were substantial in 1989, with large orders received from the former Soviet Union, Algeria and Japan. The choice of rock drill products expanded in 1989 with the addition of a rotary blast-hole drill for surface mining and quarry applications and a new hydraulic crawler line. Part of that line included the

Right: At Chek Lap Kok Island, the site of Hong Kong's future airport, these large rotary blast-hole drills are used in the displacement of 90 million cubic meters of rock to form the airport's foundation.

LMEAC-600C, a self-contained hydraulic crawler drill that could drill blastholes with 3- to 5-inch diameters. "The unit also has Ingersoll-Rand's YH95 drifter featuring fewer moving parts, and a fully automated drill-steel changing system for easy one-man operation. The carousel holds six 12-foot rods for a drilling depth capability of 82 feet with production capabilities maximized through the use of a 900-millimeter extendable boom."[13]

The Air Compressor Group experienced record earnings in 1989. It introduced a line of small rotary screw air compressors with new technology, making units clean and quiet, with protection against coolant leaks. This new technology was later expanded to larger units. Other new products included a centrifugal compressor line geared toward industries such as pharmaceutical, food and beverage, medical supply, electronics and textiles. As a result, manufacturing operations were expanded at the Air Compressor Group's Davidson, North Carolina, plant.

Ingersoll-Rand's high standards frequently earn official recognition. In 1987, the rock drill plant in Roanoke, Virginia, won the U.S. Senate Productivity Award, which recognized accomplishments, including a decrease in production costs, a lower rate of absenteeism and a reduced employee turnover. The Mayfield, Kentucky, plant, in operation since 1971, also earned the U.S. Senate Productivity Award in 1987 and 1988, marking the first time a company had earned three of the prestigious awards.

INGERSOLL-RAND HAS been represented in Japan since before the turn of the century. In 1900, Ingersoll-Rand compressors were used in the construction of the railway tunnel that linked Honshu and Kyushu. Ingersoll-Rand Japan was created in 1963. Torrington has a joint venture in Tokyo, and Ingersoll-Rand's two Japanese subsidiaries in 1995 are Ingersoll-Rand Ltd., based in

Japan

強力YHG-80V型ドリフタ搭載
TRG-300S スキットタイ
ケーシング径φ96mm～φ165mm
● φ90mm径大型シャンクロッド採用で耐久性アップ
● 現場状況によりエンジン駆動型（低騒音設計パワーパック採用）と電動型を選択できます
● 駆動装置の異常警報・停止システム内蔵

Tokyo, with branch offices in Kawasaki and Kobe, and Tokyo Ryuki Seizo Company, Ltd., with the main office in Tokyo and a factory in Yokohama.

Ingersoll-Rand helps shape the world by supplying equipment for important infrastructure projects, such as this road, under construction in Japan with the help of an SPF60 Pad Foot compactor.

CHAPTER FOURTEEN

SHAPING THE WORLD

"In its own way, Ingersoll-Rand set a piece of diplomatic history this summer [1992] when it signed a joint-venture agreement for the manufacture of air-powered tools in Russia. In so doing, Ingersoll-Rand became the first Western company to establish a joint venture to manufacture and sell air-powered tools in the former Soviet Union."

— Ingersoll-Rand *World Report*

FROM THE BEGINNING, Ingersoll-Rand has been a truly international company, selling products and services throughout the world. In the nineties, the company has entered into a number of joint ventures that have allowed it to expand its international presence as never before. From success amid the upheaval of the former Soviet Union, to supplying machinery used in the construction of a massive hydroelectric plant in China, Ingersoll-Rand has managed the bureaucratic and cultural difficulties of conducting business in the new world order.

Germany

In 1990, Ingersoll-Rand's Torrington division formed a joint venture with Georg Mueller Nuernberg AG (GMN) of West Germany to produce ball bearings in the United States. Four years later, in 1994, Ingersoll-Rand acquired GMN's interest in this joint venture, which is now wholly-owned by Ingersoll-Rand.

In October 1990, the company acquired ABG of Hameln, Germany, a manufacturer of machinery for building and repairing roads. ABG's machinery line included pavers, pavement milling machines and compactors, products that complemented other Ingersoll-Rand road machinery

equipment. These products enabled Ingersoll-Rand to build or repair virtually any road, including airport runways, and firmly established the company's ability to serve Europe's road construction contractors.

In 1993, Ingersoll-Rand acquired the assets of the Künsebeck, Germany, needle and cylindrical bearing business of FAG Kugelfischer Georg Schäfer AG of Schweinfurt, Germany, for $42.5 million. Now known as Torrington Nadellager GmbH, the acquisition contributes to Ingersoll-Rand's position in the European bearings market.

In August 1994, the company acquired the sales and service arm of Ecoair, a subsidiary of MAN Gutehoffnungshütte AG (MAN GHH), based in Oberhausen, Germany. At the same time, it formed a 50-50 joint-venture company called GHH-RAND Schraubenkompressoren. The joint venture developed and manufactured rotary screw air-ends, a major component in some industrial air compressors. "We expect these transactions to provide an increased market

---

Above: Directional drilling, introduced by Ingersoll-Rand's Klemm subsidiary, is useful in establishing river crossings, as depicted in this 1992 Amsterdam project.

Asphalt paving equipment and other road-building machinery from the Hameln, Germany, ABG plant, acquired in 1990, strengthened Ingersoll-Rand's European market position for these products.

1990 — Joint venture established between Torrington and Georg Mueller Nuernberg Ag of West Germany.

1991 — Rescue drill saves the lives of 26 miners in South Africa.

1990 — French firm of Societe Ateliers Mecaniques, Industries et Industries Agricoles is acquired.

1992 — Industrias del Rodamiento of Spain is acquired.

share for our company in Germany, as well as give us access to a broader range of air compressor technology," said Paul Bergren, president of the Air Compressor Group.[1] Chairman, President and CEO James Perrella explained that Ingersoll-Rand had been interested in forming a partnership with GHH for many years.

"We spent a good decade and a half talking to GHH — Germany's number one name in process compressors — about forming some sort of partnership. Also, GHH owned Ecoair, an air compressor sales and manufacturing company, with a strong market position in Germany. Time after time, GHH politely declined our offer, but we kept at it.

"Then, late last year, GHH experienced some financial difficulties, so we offered our aid and emerged a winner two ways. First, we bought 100 percent ownership of Ecoair to gain market strength in Germany. Second, we formed a joint venture with GHH that gave us access to some critical new technology and manufacturing capacity for compressor airends.

"In short, by being patient for 15 years or so, we were able to achieve a sudden, stunning

An ABG paver, built in Hameln, Germany, places a soil-cement base course for a new section of the Delaware Turnpike. Ingersoll-Rand compactors, built in Shippensburg, Pennsylvania, finish compacting the base.

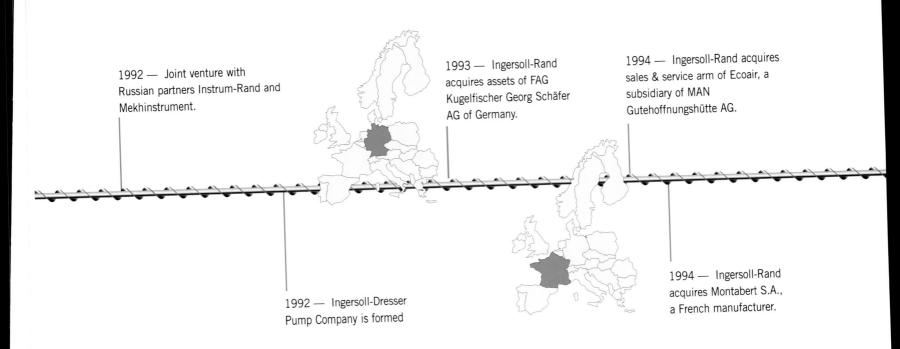

1992 — Joint venture with Russian partners Instrum-Rand and Mekhinstrument.

1993 — Ingersoll-Rand acquires assets of FAG Kugelfischer Georg Schäfer AG of Germany.

1994 — Ingersoll-Rand acquires sales & service arm of Ecoair, a subsidiary of MAN Gutehoffnungshütte AG.

1992 — Ingersoll-Dresser Pump Company is formed

1994 — Ingersoll-Rand acquires Montabert S.A., a French manufacturer.

high-performance assembly and industrial tools, adding this product line to Ingersoll-Rand's Production Equipment Group.

Russia

On July 14, 1992, Ingersoll-Rand entered a joint-venture agreement with Russian companies Gaz and Mekhinstruments. Ingersoll-Rand invested $4 million and acquired a 14 percent ownership of the new company, Instrum-Rand, noted *Ingersoll-Rand World Report.*

"In its own way, Ingersoll-Rand set a piece of diplomatic history this summer when it signed a joint-venture agreement for the manufacture of air-powered tools in Russia. In so doing, Ingersoll-Rand became the first Western company to establish a joint venture to manufacture and sell air-powered tools in the former Soviet Union. Ingersoll-Rand's Russian partners in the new joint venture, called Instrum-Rand, include GAZ, based in Nizhny Novgorod (formerly called Gorky) and Mekhin-strument, located in Pavlovo, 50 miles south of Nizhny Novgorod." [22]

Financial and political upheaval in the former Soviet Union has made it difficult to do business in the new Commonwealth of Independent States, said Carlo Piva, who is in charge of the venture.

"After we went ahead with this venture, the old Soviet world fell to pieces. The economy was heavily affected by whatever has happened. ... Nevertheless, we kept sending our Russian products, and meantime, we diversified our activity to become a supplier of componentry to our Athens, Pennsylvania and Lasunlane, United Kingdom, factories." [23]

The company also makes a rotor made of steel that is manufactured with very high tolerances, Piva said. "Ingersoll-Rand appreciates the fact that we can develop state-of-the-art products here in Russia, which is difficult to believe, but it's true." The greatest challenge, he said, is working with the complicated Russian bureaucracy. "There is nothing or very

I N 1921, INGERSOLL-RAND formed Ingersoll-Rand (India) Private Limited, one of the earliest American subsidiaries in India. Originally, the subsidiary was set up in Calcutta. Then in 1963, the head office was moved from Calcutta to Bombay. The first manufacturing plant was set up in 1965 at Naroda Ahmedabad.

In 1977, 24 percent of the equity of the subsidiary was offered to the Indian public. Capital from this offering allowed the company to establish the Naroda plant and, in 1978, establish a new facility at Bangalore.

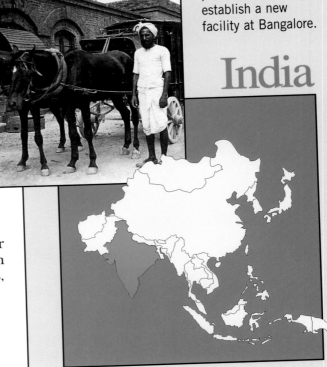

India

Ingersoll-Rand (India) Ltd. is the largest exporter of compressors in India, exporting more than 30,000 units to the United States, Canada, the United Kingdom, Italy and the Commonwealth of Independent States, formerly known as the Soviet Union.

In 1994, additional manufacturing facilities were added in Naroda to produce process gas compressors and chemical process pumps. Today, Ingersoll-Rand (India) is the oldest American company doing business there.

little done by the government to make it easier for foreigners," he said.[24]

India

In 1994, the Bearings and Components Group formed a joint venture in India with NRB-Torrington Pvt. Ltd., to produce wide inner ring ball bearings units, commonly used in conveyors, fans and blowers, under the Fafnir brand name. In November 1994, the companies agreed to merge their European steering-column production operations.[25]

An article in the *Ingersoll-Rand World Report* described some of the cultural differences between Asia and the West.

"In India, for example, it is very possible that the next shipment of parts will arrive on a cart, pulled by a water buffalo. A combination of a Western business and an Asian culture is a combination that has proved durable and successful."[26]

The Global Market

A joint venture between Ingersoll-Rand's Waterjet Cutting Systems Division and ABB Robotics was forged in 1991, creating ABB Ingersoll-Rand Robotized Waterjet AB, based in Sweden. "This joint venture represents a significant opportunity to expand the technology and installations of robotized waterjet cutting throughout Europe," said R. Barry Uber, vice president.

"We are especially proud to enter a partnership with ABB Robotics because it is the worldwide leader in robotics technology. In addition, its strong European presence will combine with Ingersoll-Rand's expertise in waterjet cutting systems to ensure technological and market leadership in this specialized field."[27]

In 1992, the company acquired Industrias del Rodamiento, S.A. (IRSA) of Spain for $14 million in cash and $1.8 million in notes. IRSA manufactures and markets an extensive line of bearings, as well as wheel kits and automotive accessories.

In 1991, Ingersoll-Rand's Waterjet Cutting Systems Division forged a joint venture with ABB Robotics in order to robotize waterjet cutting throughout Europe. This 1987 photograph shows the process before the new technology was utilized.

In 1994, a contract was signed between Ingersoll-Rand and CPM Singapore with Liyang Zhengchang Grain, Oil, & Feed Machinery. The new joint venture would come to be known as CPM Zhengchang Liyang Machinery Company Limited. It was set up to assemble and sell pellet mills, as well as manufacture machine dies and related items.

Also in 1994, Ingersoll-Rand entered an agreement with Voest-Alpine Industrieanlagenbau GmbH of Linz, Austria, to become a majority owner of a new pulping systems joint venture, which will provide integrated pulping systems to pulp producers throughout the world.[28]

Roads Around the World

Ingersoll-Rand has made the world easier to travel with a network of highways constructed with Ingersoll-Rand products. In 1993 Ingersoll-Rand cluster drills were brought in to work on the construction of an interchange on a highway from Mecca to Riyadh in Saudi Arabia.

"The project had fallen six months behind schedule before drilling began in November 1992 at the site of the interchange, located in front of the royal palaces in Riyadh. But the Ingersoll-Rand cluster drills performed far in

In 1993, this extremely efficient Ingersoll-Rand Cluster drill dramatically shortened construction time for a major expressway in Riyadh, Saudi Arabia.

Ingersoll-Rand's air-powered and hydraulic crawler drills get an early start on a day's work with the help of its portable light towers, which illuminate the construction zone from out of the camera's view.

excess of expectations, and by May 1993, the drilling phase was ahead of schedule by two weeks. In addition to supplying one CD24 and one CD40 cluster drill, the Roanoke plant supplied associated tooling, two in-line lubricators and two 30-ton capacity air swivels. Portable compressors to power the cluster drills were supplied by Ingersoll-Rand's Hindley Green plant in the United Kingdom."[29]

Saving Lives

Ingersoll-Rand products have saved lives and improved living conditions around the world. In 1990, Ingersoll-Rand's Small Air Compressor Group donated ChargeAir Pro home compressor

A common sight wherever highway or bridge work is performed, Ingersoll-Rand portable air compressors provide a convenient power source for operating a wide range of construction tools and equipment. Manufactured at plants in the United States and England, these portable air compressors are available in a broad selection of sizes, performance capabilities and special features to accommodate virtually any requirement throughout the world.

units to run equipment for two dental clinics in the Dominican Republic. Another relief organization that benefited from Ingersoll-Rand compressors was the Mercy Ships program in Jamaica. In Glasgow, Scotland, the Beatson Institute for cancer research used an Ingersoll-Rand reciprocating compressor for two decades. Compressed air is necessary for the growth of tissue cultures in research. In 1992, the compressor was retired, with an impeccable work record of no breakdowns, and replaced with the Ingersoll-Rand ML-11 SSR rotary screw compressor. The SSR rotary screw air compressor won the Product of the Year award in 1991 from *Plant Engineering* magazine.

After the Chicago River overflowed in 1992, the city of Chicago relied on Ingersoll-Rand pumps, portable generators, air compressors and light towers to help clean up the damaged city. The generators provided power to buildings and activated traffic lights that had failed during the devastating floods.

In 1995, Ingersoll-Rand Type 30 air compressors were used on board a DC-10 airplane that had been converted to a flying hospital that treats ailments in Third World countries. The compressors, donated by Ingersoll-Rand, are used to supply oxygen during on-board procedures, and to provide air that powers cutting instruments during surgery.[30]

Ingersoll-Rand's utility hammer can handle a wide variety of medium-duty demolition work, such as knocking down walls and masonry and breaking up bridge decking. The hammer, which provides the highest power-to-weight ratio ever recorded for a tool of its class, is also used for digging tunnels, as well as certain mining and quarry applications.

CHAPTER FIFTEEN

CREATING A BETTER TOMORROW

"Because it is true that the success of any business depends on its people, I am confident that our company's finest achievements remain ahead."

— Chairman, President and CEO
James Perrella

A S INGERSOLL-RAND marks its 125th anniversary, it has good reason to celebrate a legacy of growth, prosperity, and unprecedented technological advance. Ingersoll-Rand products literally shape the world by helping to construct some of the most massive projects on earth. While the company might not seen glamorous to the general public, people who know Ingersoll-Rand see it in a different light, said James E. Perrella, chairman, president and chief executive officer.

"It would be nice it we could make it glamorous to those outside the company, but it's glamorous to us inside the company. We think it's glamorous to be active in building infrastructure in the United States and around the world.

"We're involved in every part of life because — in one way or another — our products contribute to economic and social progress everywhere. So we think we have a major impact on improving life for everyone."[1]

As Ingersoll-Rand looks to the future, it is increasingly concerned with preserving the quality of life, and environmental sensitivity has become more important to the company than ever.

Concern for the Environment

In 1991, Scienco Products, a newly acquired unit of Ingersoll-Rand's Pump Group, developed a flow meter with an electric pump that made it easier to control the flow of pesticides, protecting farmers from contamination. An article in *Ingersoll-Rand World Report* explained the benefits of the product.

"In the past, many farmers applied pesticides to their crops by unscrewing the top from a two and one-half gallon jug of pesticide, measuring the pesticide in a cup, and then pouring the contents of the cup into their sprayers. Sometimes, they would use a spigot to transfer the pesticide from the container into the cup. Either method was prone to accidental spillage, and both methods exposed farmers to the pesticides."[2]

New air compressor advances in 1991 included a portable air compressor driven by natural gas, which saved money and met federal air quality standards.

The company also introduced products to combat ozone depletion. In 1992, Ingersoll-Rand's Northern Research and Engineering Corporation (NREC) won a contract from the U.S. Navy to design compressors without chlorofluorocarbons (CFCs), which contribute to the erosion of the ozone layer.

Above: An engineer at the Pulp Machinery Division in Nashua, New Hampshire, refines a circuitry diagram for electronic process and instrumentation controls used in some of the division's products.

"The prototypes that the Navy has asked NREC to develop will be the first of their kind. They represent a significant milestone in the effort to produce a practical compressor alternative, not only for the Navy, but for the commercial air conditioning market. The compressors that NREC plans to design will provide the Navy with a new generation of compressors that use gases that are environmentally safer and do not seriously undermine air conditioner performance."[3]

Reducing Waste

Ingersoll-Rand has also been working to make its own facilities more environmentally sound. In the early nineties, the company challenged its facilities to decrease hazardous waste. By 1992, the company had reducing hazardous waste by 60 percent, which had the added benefit of significantly reduced disposal costs. In 1994, the company established ambitious goals for the reduction of nonhazardous waste.

"The company will: reduce the annual volume of paper and cardboard that is disposed of as trash by 1 million pounds; reduce the annual volume of wooden skids and pallets that are discarded by 900,000 pounds; and reduce the annual volume of nonhazardous industrial sludge from manufacturing processes by 500,000 gallons. In the area of recycling, Ingersoll-Rand will reclaim and reuse 600,000 pounds of metallic grinding residue annually."[4]

Tapping New Energy Supplies

Concern over dwindling energy supplies has prompted Ingersoll-Rand to find new ways to tap and preserve natural resources. Ingersoll-Rand products were critical to the 1992 construction of the pipeline connecting Alberta, Canada, and Long Island, New York. "Since this job is only increasing the capacity of the existing system," Ingersoll-Rand announced, "its completion will not result directly in any new users of natural gas. But it will contribute significantly to the energy security of North America, and, in particular, the natural gas supplies of the northeastern United States."[5]

The company's products also have been instrumental in Canada's offshore oil field development, a project that is expected to provide as much as 12 percent of Canada's light crude production by the year 2000. In 1993, Dresser-Rand Canada, Ingersoll-Rand's Construction & Mining Group, and Ingersoll-Dresser Pump Company supplied equipment for the Hibernia offshore oil project. Equipment

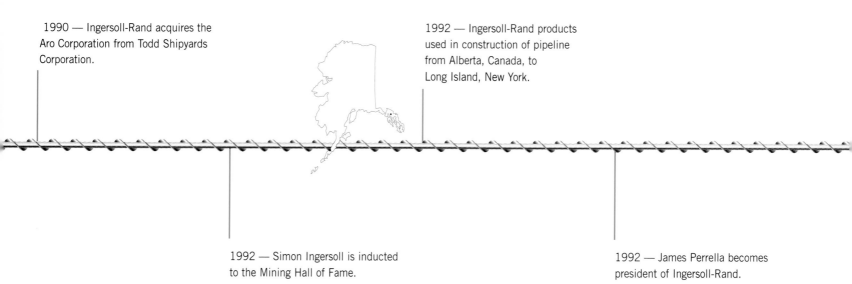

1990 — Ingersoll-Rand acquires the Aro Corporation from Todd Shipyards Corporation.

1992 — Ingersoll-Rand products used in construction of pipeline from Alberta, Canada, to Long Island, New York.

1992 — Simon Ingersoll is inducted to the Mining Hall of Fame.

1992 — James Perrella becomes president of Ingersoll-Rand.

Ingersoll-Rand supplied Crawlair drills, hydraulic drills, portable compressors and light towers for the Hibernia offshore oil project in 1993. Canada's offshore oil field development is expected to provide as much as 12 percent of Canada's light crude production by the year 2000.

supplied included Crawlair drills, hydraulic drills, portable compressors and light towers.

Safety

The company has constantly searched for ways to improve safety during manufacturing. In 1991, the Power Tool Division introduced two devices, the Ergo-Analyzer and the Interactive Task Simulator, that reduced the cumulative trauma disorder risks of the assembly-line worker.

"The Ergo-Analyzer device helps tooling engineers select a tool design and configuration that acts as an interface between the operators' physical characteristics and the requirements of particular tasks. ... As varying tool configurations are simulated and then modified, the Ergo-Analyzer helps keep the operator's wrist in a neutral position. With the dual-module Interactive Task Simulator unit, specific tasks conducted at vertical or horizontal assembly-line workstations can be re-enacted. During simulations, operator posture can be analyzed to determine appropriate tool configurations required for reducing bodily stress, such as twisting or bending, and maintaining neutral working positions."[6]

1992 — Ingersoll-Rand contracted by Navy to design refrigerator compressors without chlorofluorocarbons.

1993 — Ingersoll-Rand's new two-stage rotary air compressor is voted Best Product of the Year in *Plant Engineering* magazine.

1993 — James Perrella is elected chairman and chief executive officer of Ingersoll-Rand.

1995 — Clark Equipment Company is acquired.

The Swan Lane manufacturing plant in England received a British Safety Council National Safety Award for the 12th year in a row in 1992. To qualify, a plant must achieve a lower accident level than the targeted national average in its industry.

The Aro Corporation

In February 1990, the company made its largest acquisition in years when it purchased The Aro Corporation from Todd Shipyards Corporation for more than $131.5 million. Aro manufactures air-powered tools, valves, pumps and other related equipment, a true complement to Ingersoll-Rand's existing product lines. This group won several important contracts for Ingersoll-Rand.

During Operation Desert Storm in 1991, Aro random orbital sanders helped U.S. Army pilots see more clearly by polishing windshields used on many helicopters and small fixed-wing aircraft. The polishing kits and sanders allowed ground crews to remove scratches caused by sand.[7]

A compact unit from the Fluid Products Division can be mounted in any position without sacrificing performance. Designed to pump all types of industrial fluids, the unit earned distinction as the best fluid power product of 1993 from *Design News* magazine for its "flexibility, adaptability and versatility."

The Aro Life Support Products Division won a contract in 1993 to develop a breathing regulator for the Navy's Advanced Tactical Life Support System. When used with other equipment, the regulator combats the severe effects of "G" forces.[8]

In 1994, the Aro Fluid Products Division , located in Bryan, Ohio, was moved from Temse, Belgium, to the Tool & Hoist Division's Swan Lane factory, in Hindley Green, England.[9]

In April 1991, Ingersoll-Rand sold its North American consumer air compressor business. In 1992, Ingersoll-Rand acquired the assets of The New Centri-Spray Corporation, which was created at the end of the year. The company, based in Livonia, Michigan, manufactures heavy-duty industrial washers, deburring equipment and associated automated materials handling machinery. The company's washing systems are used primarily in the automotive and other transportation-related industries to clean machined parts.[10] These assets became part of Ingersoll-Rand's Production Equipment Group, and production continued in Livonia.

In 1994, Ingersoll-Rand acquired operating assets of the international fastener tightening business of SPS Technologies, Inc., a leading manufacturer of threaded fasteners and fastener tightening equipment for industrial assembly applications.

James E. Perrella

In September 1992, James E. Perrella was nominated president of Ingersoll-Rand. In the 90 years since Ingersoll-Sergeant Drill Company merged with the Rand Drill Company, Ingersoll-Rand has had only 12 presidents, a testimony to the stability of the company and the durability of its leadership. Perrella joined Ingersoll-Rand in 1962, after receiving a degree in mechanical engineering in 1960 and a degree in industrial management in 1961 from Purdue University.

D. Wayne Hallstein, president from 1967 to 1974, was instrumental in hiring Perrella.

"Then-CEO Robert Johnson decided to hire some engineer undergraduates with MBAs and put them on a special training program on the fast track. ... We used to hire about eight a year, and I sort of ran the training program. Jim was

one of the guys we picked up. I remember his first assignment was as controller of one of the divisions."[11]

Ted Black recognized Perrella's potential, and wasted little time in preparing him for the ultimate leadership of Ingersoll-Rand. "I started to groom Perrella probably the day I got into the chair," said Black, CEO from 1988 to 1993.

"He had a varied experience. In the five or six years I was here we put him in a number of seats. I would say he was very diligent, very earnest. He worked very hard at all of them and certainly proved that the jobs I was giving him were putting him on the road to taking the chairmanship."[12]

In 1977, Perrella became a vice president, and in 1982 he was elected to executive vice president. His responsibilities while serving as an executive vice president included Ingersoll-Rand International, the Air Compressor Group, the Tool Group, the Door Hardware Group (renamed the Architectural Hardware Group in 1995), the Pump Group, the Process Systems Group, and the Bearings and Components Group.

In 1994, Purdue University awarded Perrella an honorary doctor of engineering degree. He is also a member of the Dean's Advisory Council of Purdue's Krannert School of Management. Perrella returns to Purdue, as well as other universities, to speak about business and industry. In a

James E. Perrella has been leading Ingersoll-Rand as chairman, president and chief executive officer since November 1993. He has also been serving as president since 1992. Perrella began his career with Ingersoll-Rand in 1962. After his first year as chairman, president and CEO of Ingersoll-Rand, the company achieved new levels of success, with net sales reaching over $4.5 billion.

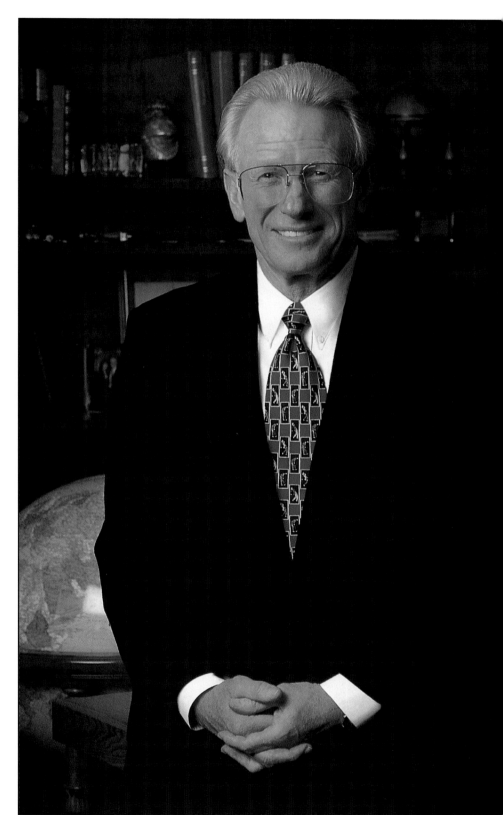

1994 speech at the University of Illinois, Perrella spoke to students about business ethics.

"Plainly stated, bad ethics just does not pay. Bad ethics is a corrosive force that ultimately destroys three things that are essential to the long-term survival of any business: public trust, public respect, and organizational efficiency."[13]

Board member Alexander Massad, former executive vice president of Mobil Oil Corporation, praised Perrella.

"Jim is an individual. He has his opinions, and he hears opinions from the board. I think one of the things we have tried to push the Ingersoll-Rand board to do is to do more forward planning, trying to get a better feel, where do you want to be, how do you want to be positioned five years from now, what areas should we be in, and how should we get there? You have to know how you're going to get there, and this is the thing that many of us have talked to executives about. Jim is very forthcoming with his thoughts."[14]

William Armstrong, vice president and treasurer, said Perrella has a different leadership style than his predecessors. "It's more of a shared responsibility. ... It's a different style than the other guys. A little bit is because he can be that way, and a little bit is because the times demand something different, more of a radical change."[15]

Al Nixon, president of Torrington, said Perrella "is involving the field in decisions. In the past, I always felt decisions were made, and then Torrington would implement them. Now, we're getting more of a voice in helping to shape those policies and those decisions."[16]

Perrella said he is working hard to bring about change at Ingersoll-Rand. "We've got a good strong company, which is great. But we can't live only on our past laurels. We've got to build for tomorrow. And to build for tomorrow, we've got to make sure we are doing those things that make customers want to buy from us."[17]

"Our people have good ideas and we must provide an atmosphere where ideas can be expressed without fear," he said. "We must engage the minds of all employees working for Ingersoll-Rand Company."[18] Perrella expressed this view in the 1993 *Annual Report.*

Above: Thomas F. McBride is senior vice president and chief financial officer of Ingersoll-Rand.

Left: William G. Mulligan, who retired in 1995, was executive vice president of Ingersoll-Rand.

"Our future competitiveness in all our markets will be predicated upon the desire to seek change, the ability to accelerate our business processes and a craving for continuous improvement. Everything we do shall be judged by whether it adds value to our customers' operations, to our company and to our shareholders'

Left to Right:

William J. Armstrong, vice president and treasurer.

Paul L. Bergren, vice president in charge of the Air Compressor Group.

Brian Jellison, president of the Architectural Hardware Group.

investment. In addition, we will focus on what we do best: engage the minds, talents and energy of all our people and continually build upon our competitive advanced technology and, especially, in our people. ... Because it is true that the success of any business depends on its people, I am confident that our company's finest achievements remain ahead." [19]

Patents

Naturally, Ingersoll-Rand has continued to develop new and innovative products. In 1991, a new record was set for the company, with 88 patents issued in a single year. In 1992, 90 patents were issued, and the following year, the number increased 35 percent, to 122. [20]

Since 1992, the company has invested more than $125 million each year on research and development. Perrella noted that it sometimes takes time for a patent to boost the company's bottom line. "Patents give us a long-term advantage," he said. "Patents of previous years still contribute to our company. The bottom line of a patent is a bet on the future, if you will. And we think that, eventually, each patent will give us the contribution we want." [21]

The company has a busy 12-person patent office that helps it obtain patents for new products. John Selko, chief of patents, explained the process.

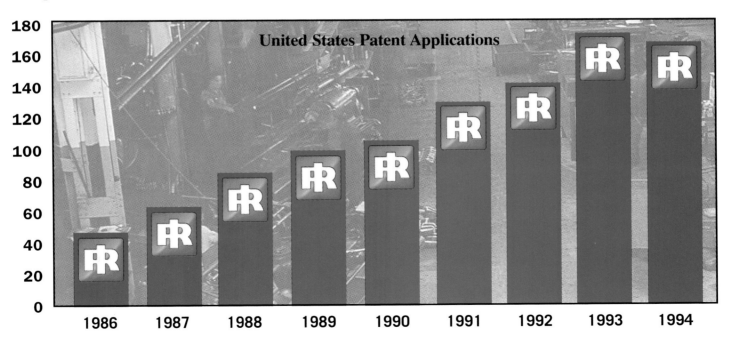

United States Patent Applications

systems. These rigs were specially designed for the military in that they could be transported without disassembly.

Among the drills introduced in 1992 were a rotary blast-hole drill, a hydraulic drifter for underground work, and a water-powered, hand-held drill for mining precious metals.

A new line of hydraulic rock drills pioneered by the Roanoke, Virginia, plant, was developed to meet North American construction, mining and quarrying needs. The Roanoke plant offered self-contained hydraulic crawler that provides increased efficiency with lower noise, less vibration and less dust. New downhole drill developments included the introduction of cluster drills that use downhole drills for the purpose of drilling caissons or foundation holes.

Perhaps the company's most impressive drills are the million-dollar rotary drills manufactured in Garland, Texas, said R. Barry Uber, president of Construction And Mining Group. "There are a lot of things that have to work together," he said. "These units have a level of complexity with hydraulics and electronics, in association with a combination of all the mechanical pieces. So you are dealing with three significant applications of engineering."[29]

The company has also been introducing items that are much smaller in scale. In 1993, Ingersoll-Rand introduced the IR2131 impact wrench, and demand has been high. "The new tool was designed in response to professional auto mechanics' desire for two things — brute force required to loosen over-tightened nuts and bolts, and torque-control features needed to prevent overtightening of nuts and bolts. Incorporating an advanced composite housing material, the new impact wrench weighs only 4.5 pounds, and offers the most compact half-inch impact wrench profile on the market."[30]

In 1993, the company introduced a two-stage rotary air compressor with the capability of providing access to high-horsepower industrial applications that were once found only in recip-rocating and centrifugal models. This new rotary unit was voted Best Product of the Year by readers of *Plant Engineering* magazine.

Clark

Ingersoll-Rand disclosed on March 28, 1995 that it had launched a $1.34 billion acquisition bid for Clark Equipment Company, based in

At a new factory in Spring Hill, Tennessee, Ingersoll-Rand's automated production systems assemble and test four-cylinder engines used in Saturn Corporation's vehicles. The wholly owned subsidiary of General Motors uses Ingersoll-Rand centrifugal air compressors, hoists, tools and pumps throughout the plant, as well as needle bearings for automatic and manual transmissions and the 1.9-liter engine.

Prevalent at large mining properties throughout the world, Ingersoll-Rand's rotary blasthole drills speed production of coal and precious metals essential to economic and industrial progress. This unit is operating at an iron ore mine in India.

 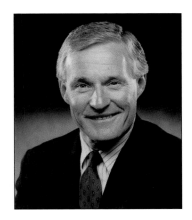

Above, left: Larry H. Pitsch, vice president in charge of the Process Systems Group.

Above right: Donald H. Rice, vice president in charge of Human Resources.

South Bend, Indiana. It was the first time Ingersoll-Rand had engaged in an acquisition without the consent of the target company.

"We realized that we weren't going to make any acquisition that was friendly," said William Mulligan. "The kind of things we were interested in buying, people were not interested in selling."[31] Mulligan, who is 1995 chairman of the American Road and Transportation Builders Association, is responsible for Ingersoll-Rand's overall merger, acquisition and divestiture efforts. Mulligan joined Ingersoll-Rand in 1952 and worked his way up through company ranks. He has been executive vice president since 1976.

Clark, which had sales of $950 million in 1994, makes highway-paving and light construction equipment. Clark responded to the bid by filing suit against Ingersoll-Rand, claiming a merger would violate antitrust laws, and rejected the offer of $75 to $77 a share.[32] Clark stock rose from $53.12 to $83.25 by March 30. On April 3, Perrella wrote a letter to Leo McKernan, chairman, president and CEO of Clark, offering $77 per share.[33]

Clark's CEO McKernan responded that Ingersoll-Rand's offer was "entirely inadequate," noting that Clark stock hit $71 in November. But a week later, on April 10, Clark accepted an offer of $86 a share, for a total of $1.46 billion. With this newest acquisition, Ingersoll-Rand has combined sales of nearly $5.5 billion and more than 45,000 employees.

The Clark Equipment Company was founded in 1903 as the George M. Rich Manufacturing Company when executives of the Illinois Steel Company in Chicago invented a drill strong enough to bore steel railroad rails, and formed a small company in the basement to furnish the drills to themselves. They hired a consultant named Eugene B. Clark, who wound up as manager of the company, which he renamed Celfor Tool Company, after the drill that was sold. In 1916, Celfor Tool Company merged with

Buchanan Electric Steel Company to form Clark Equipment Company.

In 1917, the company developed a shop buggy, dubbed the TrucTractor. "It was a three-wheeled, gas-powered vehicle. In its first form, it wasn't much of a design. To go right, the driver steered left. To go left, he steered right. To stop quickly, he had to run into something because the vehicle had no brakes."[34] But it did the job, and Clark established the Clark TrucTractor Company. In the early twenties, the first platform lift truck was introduced.

Clark went public in 1928, when sales were nearly $12 million and earnings were $1.2 million. In 1934, Clark began to manufacture rivets and it developed a pneumatic gun for setting them. During World War II, the company made as many as 2,500 vehicles a month, a huge increase from the 50 to 75 vehicles per month it had sold previously. By 1943, Clark sales had grown to $77 million. In the late fifties, the company began an acquisition strategy that included the purchase of the Brown Trailer Company in 1959 and Tyler Refrigeration in 1961.

The Bobcat Skid-Steer (above left), the Club Car golf cart (above) and the Blaw-Knox paver (opposite bottom) are among the products that made Clark a desirable acquisition for Ingersoll-Rand.

In an interview after the acquisition, Perrella said Clark fit the Ingersoll-Rand profile of a desirable acquisition.

"We set a strategy that said we were going to evaluate companies of significant size, not exactly in our same business, but in businesses that we understood and could make a contribution to. We conducted a search process on the basis of companies that had a good financial performance. ... So, we went through our sorting process, and we must have gone through hundreds of companies during that process. We had also established a target that we considered appropriate to have an impact on our company, above five hundred million, and we didn't really want to go over a billion. And Clark kept coming up, kept coming up."[35]

He noted that Clark became even more attractive to Ingersoll-Rand after it sold its 50 percent stake in VME Group NV, a construction equipment maker, to joint venture partner AB Volvo for $573 million. Another positive aspect of the Clark acquisition was that it had purchased Club Car, the number two golf cart manufacturer, for $235 million in 1995. Noted Perrella: "Club Car golf carts and light utility vehicles have no direct complement with Ingersoll-Rand, but the Club Car business is positioned to benefit from the surging interest in golf around the world."[36]

Clark had also purchased Blaw-Knox Construction Equipment Corporation in 1994. At the 1995 shareholder meeting, CEO Perrella noted that the Clark acquisition gives Ingersoll-Rand the opportunity to explore new markets.

"Clark's highly regarded products now include Bobcat skid steer loaders and mini excavators, and Spra-Coupe agricultural sprayers. These

Left to right: Gerald E. Swimmer, vice president in charge of Taxes and Financial Administrative Services; R. Barry Uber, vice president in charge of the Construction Equipment Group; Ronald G. Heller, secretary; Dick Johnson, executive director of Public Affairs.

products provide Ingersoll-Rand the opportunity to pursue a major expansion of product lines for agricultural and construction markets. In particular, the Bobcat products are well positioned for growth in connection with the trend toward use of smaller and lighter construction equipment. ... We are especially enthusiastic about our ability to widen distribution of the Bobcat, Spra-Coupe and Blaw-Knox product lines into the Asia-Pacific region and Europe."[37]

CFO Tom McBride said the acquisition "would have been an impossibility in this company 10 years ago. But we're a much stronger company, financially, today. We have a very strong balance sheet, which was not the case 10 years ago. ... We would never have been in a position to leverage a company to make this kind of acquisition."[38]

When Ingersoll-Rand acquired the company, it acquired a reserve of half a billion dollars in cash. McBride and General Counsel Patricia Nachtigal both said Ingersoll-Rand is not particularly vulnerable to a takeover because of its growing size and strategically balanced debt-to-capitalization ratio. "We probably quadrupled the market capitalization of this company since 1985," McBride said. "And each step along that way, we became a little less vulnerable."[39]

Ingersoll-Rand and Clark share many similarities, Perrella reflected.

The Intermodal Surface Transportation Efficiency Act of 1991, proposed by President George Bush, appeared hopelessly snarled in Congress. Sensing the need to remind lawmakers of the link between efficient transportation systems and economic growth, Ingersoll-Rand's Construction and Mining Group rapidly deployed a program called "Build for the Future," to enlist support for the transportation bill among customers, distributors, employees and Congress. The effort included issuing news bulletins relating to negotiations, establishing a hot-line to field questions from customers and employees, and urging interested parties to write to members of Congress and administration officials. Also, Ingersoll-Rand executives met with influential lawmakers. After Congress reached a compromise on the bill in December 1991, President Bush signed the bill into law, providing, over a six-year period, $119.5 billion for highway projects, and $31.5 billion for mass-transit spending. While Ingersoll-Rand was reluctant to take credit for the bill's passage, the company's initiative ensured that the voices of its distributors, customers and employees were heard.

"Their culture is made up of people who are mechanical engineers. It's made up of people who graduated from the same kinds of colleges that our people came from. They develop almost all of their people from within. They have a few outside people that came in, as we do. But mostly, it's a culture of mechanical engineers who come in from scratch and work themselves up through the organization. So I'd say in that sense they have a similar culture. They also market their products throughout the world, like we do."[40]

R. Barry Uber, president of Ingersoll-Rand's Construction and Mining Group, said, "Clark has put together a portfolio of businesses that all are independently operated, and all have improved performances."[41]

Clark's international business is not as large as Ingersoll-Rand's, so "we can give them an extra boost in doing some international business," Perrella added. "I think they're going to give us some extra boost too. It's going to be a sharing on both sides, helping each other in the process."[42]

Before the deal could be sanctioned by the Federal Trade Commission, Ingersoll-Rand had

to divest a $10 million paving company, Perrella said. On May 15, 1995, the company announced that it had sold its domestic Paving Equipment Business to Champion Road Machinery Limited of Canada.[43]

Nachtigal added that changes in the individual companies will be minor.

"Nothing will change, I think. Nothing material as far as the operations of the business except for the better, and as far as the headquarters, yes I realize there will be change. I mean we really don't need two headquarters. But I think their management made very sound arrangements for [displaced employees] by way of settlements, and I think within the time period they have for their severance and benefits, they will find other jobs."[44]

"I think what we see now in Jim [Perrella] is more of a visionary. I think he, in this recent acquisition, demonstrated that," said board member Alexander Massad.[45]

The Future

Mining and construction will be a much stronger performer for the company in the next five or 10 years, predicted Uber.

"I'd say it will be less cyclical than we have seen in the past. We will work on all our internal processes to be able to shorten our lead time for everything, which will allow us to respond better to the market with less inventory, and therefore have a much better return on assets in the future. I think there are segments of the market we should expand. There's a market growth both in existing products where we can get share, and some extensions of products that will allow us to serve a broader segment of the markets that we're in."[46]

Jim Lahey, director of Total Quality Leadership, said the company is more flexible than it has been in the past.

"We will be around 50 years from now because of our ability to discard what doesn't work. We're getting better at that. We're getting better at discarding management practices that worked for us 30 years ago, or even 20 years ago, but no longer work for us. We're getting better in the product area of really going out and hearing the voice of the customer, really trying to understand what they want. Twenty years ago we were an engineering organization that would engineer a great product and then sell it to you. We are becoming a learning organization."[47]

In 1991, this commitment to quality was recognized when the Ford Motor Company awarded the Torrington division of Ingersoll-Rand Canada Inc. with the Q1 Preferred Quality Award, which has become synonymous with their slogan, "Quality is job one." To receive this award, a company must display quality at all levels of manufacturing. To remain a Ford supplier, the company must retain a Q1 status.

"The Ford Q1 evaluation process pays particular attention to a supplier's ability to maintain quality while implementing new manufacturing processes. Other key aspects of the Q1 certification process include a commitment by the supplier's management to continuous improvement and management's ability to track key indicators."[48]

In a 1992 speech, James Perrella said Ingersoll-Rand cannot rest on its reputation for high quality, but must always strive to do better.

"Since our very early years, even before Ingersoll and Rand joined forces, our people have focused on quality to win customers. I believe, however, that the standard of quality is increasingly more demanding; therefore, we must, each year, keep reaching to higher standards of quality."[49]

In a recent interview, he reinforced the point.

"I'm looking for improvement. I want to create an atmosphere where people are pleased with the progress they're making, but they're dissatisfied with what they've done today compared with what they feel can be accomplished tomorrow. If we can get that kind of philosophy throughout the organization, we'll really get one hell of a company. And it's moving. It isn't there, but it's moving. It takes constant energy from all the officers of the company, and all the management of the company to keep this process going. And we'll be stronger. We're going to be a different company."[50]

In a speech to shareholders April 27, 1995, Perrella noted that the company has continued along this course of positive change.

"Since I assumed stewardship of our company, I have emphasized the need for dramatic change throughout Ingersoll-Rand. This need is driven by an obsession to serve our customers more effectively and more efficiently. I am pleased to say that Ingersoll-Rand people have embraced the challenge to implement change now, while our company is in a position of strength."[51]

NOTES TO SOURCES

Chapter One

1. C.H. Vivian, *The Ingersoll-Rand Story 1871-1964.* vol. 1, Early Mechanical Rock Drills, 1966, p. 13. The extensive work of C.H. Vivian has been a valuable resource for this history. Vivian, the editor of *Compressed Air Magazine* for more than 20 years, compiled the history of Ingersoll- Rand into eight bound volumes, each more than five inches thick. Each volume is divided into several sections, all numbered from page one forward, as reflected in the source notes here. The project was completed in 1966.
2. *The Ingersoll-Rand Story.* vol. 3, Leyner Drills, p. 1.
3. George Koether, *The Building of Men, Machines and a Company.* Reprinted from *Compressed Air Magazine*, (Ingersoll-Rand: 1971), p. 12.
4. *Ibid.*, p. 13.
5. "Company Founder Inducted into Mining Hall of Fame," Ingersoll-Rand World Report, 1992.
6. James T. Johnson, "Ingersoll-Rand," *New Jersey History of Ingenuity and Industry.* (Windsor Publications:1987).
7. *Men, Machines and a Company*, 17.
8. *Ibid.*, 25.
9. *Men, Machines and a Company*, 25.
10. *Ibid.*, 20-21.
11. *Ibid.*, 21-22.
12. *The Ingersoll-Rand Story.* vol. 1, Origin and Development of the Ingersoll Branch, p. 6.
13. *Ibid.*, 10.
14. *The Ingersoll-Rand Story.* vol. 1, Origin and Development of the Ingersoll Branch, p. 21.
15. *The Ingersoll-Rand Story.* vol. 1, Ingersoll Rock Drills, p. 11.
16. *The Ingersoll Rand Story.* vol. 1, Origin and Development of the Ingersoll Branch, pp. 46-47.
17. Marquis James, *Merchant Adventurer. The Story of W.R. Grace.* (W.R. Grace & Co.: 1993), pp. 152-153.
18. *Ibid.*, pp. 295-296.
19. Quoted in *Grace: W.R. Grace & Co. The Formative Years 1850-1930*, Lawrence A. Clayton. (Jameson Books: Ottawa, Illinois, 1985), p. 265.
20. *The Ingersoll-Rand Story.* vol. 8, Ingersoll-Rand Company Limited, p. 1.
21. *The Ingersoll-Rand Story.* vol. 8, West Germany, p. 1.
22. *The Ingersoll-Rand Story.* vol. 8, Japan, p. 1.

Chapter Two

1. George Koether, *The Building of Men, Machines*

and a Company. Reprinted from *Compressed Air Magazine*, (Ingersoll-Rand: 1971), p. 62.

2. *Ibid.*, p. 65.
3. *Ibid.*, p. 66.
4. C.H. Vivian, *The Ingersoll-Rand Story 1871-1964.* vol. 1, Rand Rock Drills, 1966, p. 1.
5. *Men, Machines and a Company*, p. 72.
6. *The Ingersoll-Rand Story.* vol. 1, Rand Rock Drills, p. 11.
7. *The Ingersoll-Rand Story.* vol. 1, Formation and Growth of Rand Drill Company, p. 2.
8. *Ibid.*, p. 40.
9. *The Ingersoll-Rand Story.* vol. 1, Early Mechanical Rock Drills, p. 4.
10. *The Ingersoll-Rand Story.* vol. 2, Ingersoll Compressors, p. 1.
11. *The Ingersoll-Rand Story.* vol. 2, Rand Compressors, p. 6.
12. *The Ingersoll-Rand Story.* vol. 1, Painted Post Plant, p. 1.

Chapter Three

1. C.H. Vivian, *The Ingersoll-Rand Story 1871-1964.* vol. 8, Australia, 1966, p. 1.
2. *The Ingersoll-Rand Story.* vol. 8, South Africa, p. 2.
3. *The Ingersoll-Rand Story.* vol. 2, Quality, p. 1.

4. *The Ingersoll-Rand Story.* vol. 1, Construction of Easton, Pa., Factory, p. 2.
5. *The Ingersoll-Rand Story.* vol. 1, Construction of Phillipsburg Factory, p. 7.
6. *The Ingersoll-Rand Story.* vol. 1, Construction of Easton, Pa., Factory, p. 6.
7. *The Ingersoll-Rand Story.* vol. 3, Calyx Core Drills, p. 2.
8. *The Ingersoll-Rand Story.* vol. 3, Temple-Ingersoll Drill, p. 5.
9. *Ibid.*, p. 10.
10. *The Ingersoll-Rand Story.* vol. 5, Portable Compressors, p. 2-3.
11. *The Ingersoll-Rand Story.* vol. 2, Rand Compressors, p. 33.
12. *The Ingersoll-Rand Story.* vol. 3, Temple-Ingersoll Drill, p. 3.
13. *Ibid.*, p. 10.
14. *The Ingersoll-Rand Story.* vol. 4, Corliss Compressors, p. 1.
15. *Ibid.*
16. *The Ingersoll-Rand Story.* vol. 2, Phillipsburg-Easton from 1904 Onward, p. 9-13.
17. *Ibid.*
18. *The Ingersoll-Rand Story.* vol. 1, Rand Rock Drills, p. 13.
19. *The Ingersoll-Rand Story.* vol. 1, Early Drill Advertisements, pp.4-5.
20. *The Ingersoll-Rand Story.* vol. 2, Birth of Ingersoll-

Rand Company, p. 1.
21. *The Ingersoll-Rand Story.* vol. 2, Birth of Ingersoll-Rand Company,p. 19.

Chapter Four

1. George Koether, *The Building of Men, Machines and a Company.* Reprinted from *Compressed Air Magazine*, (Ingersoll-Rand: 1971), pp. 106-107.
2. C.H. Vivian, *The Ingersoll-Rand Story 1871-1964.* vol. 2, Birth of Ingersoll-Rand Company, 1966, p. 8.
3. *The Ingersoll-Rand Story.* vol. 2, Birth of Ingersoll-Rand Company, p. 12.
4. James Perrella, *Changing the Way We Do Things*, a speech given before the Purchasing and Quality Councils, Charlotte, North Carolina, November 10, 1992. Transcript, p. 4.
5. *The Ingersoll-Rand Story.* vol. 4, Ingersoll-Rand Compressors, p. 2.
6. *Men, Machines and a Company.*, p. 76.
7. William Saunders, "The Big Little Rock Drill," undated, found in company archives.
8. *The Ingersoll-Rand Story.* vol. 2, Birth of Ingersoll-Rand Company, p. 20.
9. *Ibid.*, p. 15.

10. *Ibid.*, pp. 28-29.
11. James Perrella, *Going Where the Customers Are, Worldwide*, a speech given at the International Management Seminar, Compagnie de Saint-Gobain, St. Michaels, Maryland, September 11, 1995. Transcript, p. 4.
12. Daniel Kletter, interviewed by the author, May 2, 1995, Woodcliff Lake, New Jersey. Transcript, p. 31
13. *The Ingersoll-Rand Story.* vol. 2, Patents, p. 3.
14. D. Wayne Hallstein, interviewed by the author, April 27, 1995, Woodcliff Lake, New Jersey. Transcript, p. 24.
15. *The Ingersoll-Rand Story.* vol. 4, Electric-Driven Compressors, p. 1.
16. *Ibid.*, p. 6.
17. *The Ingersoll-Rand Story.* vol. 4, Classes E and F, p. 2.
18. *The Ingersoll-Rand Story.* vol. 6, Cameron Pumps, p. 1.
19. *The Ingersoll-Rand Story.* vol. 3, Advertising and Publicity , p. 1.
20. *Ibid.*, p. 4.
21. *Ibid.*, p. 22.

Chapter Five

1. J. Peter Grace, interviewed by the author, March 14, 1995.
2. C.H. Vivian, *The Ingersoll-Rand Story 1871-1964.* vol. 2, Chief Executives, 1966, pp. 3-4.
3. "Johnson and Hopton of Ingersoll-Rand," *Forbes,* July 1, 1965, p. 20.
4. Story by Walter Leutwyler, in G-Rand Times, December 8, 1989, p. 15.
5. *The Ingersoll-Rand Story,* vol. 2, Chief Executives, pp. 2-4.
6. *The Ingersoll-Rand Story.* vol. 4, Leyner Compressors, pp. 2-3.
7. *Ibid.*
8. *The Ingersoll-Rand Story.* vol. 3, Evolution of the 'Jackhamer,' p. 46.
9. King Cunningham, interviewed by the author, November 17, 1994, Woodcliff Lake, New Jersey. Transcript, p. 60.
10. William Austin, interviewed by the author, November 17, 1994, Woodcliff Lake, New Jersey. Transcript, p. 60.
11. *The Ingersoll-Rand Story.* vol. 4, Drifter Drills, p. 12.
12. *The Ingersoll-Rand Story.* vol. 4, Wagon Drills, p. 1.
13. *The Ingersoll-Rand Story.* vol. 3, Submarine Drilling, p. 1.
14. *Ibid.*, p. 10.
15. *The Ingersoll-Rand Story,* vol. 7, Pneumatic Tie Tamping, pp. 3-4.
16. *Ibid.*
17. *The Ingersoll-Rand Story.* vol. 5, Type XPV, p. 1.
18. *The Ingersoll-Rand Story.* vol. 4, Classes E and F, p. 4.
19. *The Ingersoll-Rand Story.* vol. 5, Portable Compressors, p. 35.
20. *Ibid.*
21. *The Ingersoll-Rand Story.* vol. 2, Phillipsburg-Easton, from 1904 Onward, pp. 9-13.
22. *The Ingersoll-Rand Story.* vol. 5, Refrigeration Compressors, pp 2-3.
23. *The Ingersoll-Rand Story.* vol. 7, The Oil Electric Locomotive, pp. 12-13.
24. King Cunningham, interviewed by the author, November 17 1994, Woodcliff Lake, New Jersey. Transcript, p. 19.
25. *The Ingersoll-Rand Story.* vol. 5, Gas Compressors, pp 1-2.
26. *The Ingersoll-Rand Story.* vol. 5, Gas Engine Compressors, p. 11.
27. *Ibid.*, pp. 26-28.

Chapter Six

1. C.H. Vivian, *The Ingersoll-Rand Story 1871-1964* vol. 2, Chief Executives, 1966, pp. 2-4.
2. *The Ingersoll-Rand Story.* vol. 5, Type 30, p. 3.
3. H. Kirk Lewis, interviewed by the author, April 19, 1995., Woodcliff Lake, New Jersey. Transcript, p. 8.

4. *The Ingersoll-Rand Story.* vol. 2, Chief Executives, p. 3.
5. "Ingersoll-Rand Company Significant Trends Since Incorporation," *memo.* January 26, 1994.
6. Copeland Lake, "Construction of the Hoover Dam," *The Story of the Hoover Dam.* (Nevada Publications: Las Vegas, Nevada), p. 60. Reprinted from articles in *Compressed Air Magazine*, 1931-1935.
7. *The Ingersoll-Rand Story.* vol. 5, Electric and Belt-Driven Units, 1910-65, p. 7.
8. *The Ingersoll-Rand Story.* vol. 2, Chief Executives, p. 5.
9. *The Ingersoll-Rand Story.* vol. 4, Electric-Driven Compressors, p. 16.
10. *The Ingersoll-Rand Story.* vol. 5, High-Pressure Compressors, p. 29.
11. *The Ingersoll-Rand Story.* vol. 2, Philipsburg-Easton, from 1904 Onward, pp. 9-13.
12. *The Ingersoll-Rand Story.* vol. 2, World War II Service, p. 2.

Chapter Seven

1. H. Kirk Lewis, interviewed by the author, April 19, 1995, Woodcliff Lake, New Jersey. Transcript, p. 3.
2. Joe Wiendl, interviewed by the author, November 17, 1994, Woodcliff Lake, New Jersey. Transcript, p. 4.
3. King Cunningham, interviewed by the author, November 17, 1994, Woodcliff Lake, New Jersey. Transcript, p. 23.
4. Bill Austin, interviewed by the author, November 17, 1995, Woodcliff Lake, New Jersey. Transcript, p. 23.
5. Austin interview, p. 25.
6. "The Association's Origins and Purposes," *The G-Rand Times,* published by the G-Men's Association, somewhere in Texas, December 8, 1989, p. 2.
7. Story by Doyle Reynolds, told by Sue McMillan in *The G-Rand Times,* December 8, 1989, p. 14.
8. *The G-Rand Times,* August 13, 1990, p. 6.
9. Richard Kniffen, interviewed by the author, November 17, 1995, Woodcliff Lake, New Jersey. Transcript, p. 34.
10. Story by H. Kirk Lewis, *G-Rand Times,* August 13, 1990, p. 12.
11. *Ibid.,* p. 13.
12. Story by H. Kirk Lewis, *G-Rand Times,* December 8, 1989, p. 16.
13. Wiendl interview, p. 5.
14. Ibid., p. 27.
15. W.E. Austin, *Don't Do As I Say...Do What Works!,* 1982.
16. David C. Garfield, interviewed by the author, December 30, 1994. Transcript, p. 6.
17. Story by Jack Zoeller, *G-Rand Times,* December 8, 1989, p. 16.
18. Story by H. Kirk Lewis, *G-Rand Times,* December 8, 1989, p. 16.
19. C.H. Vivian, *The Ingersoll-Rand Story 1871-1964.* vol. 4, The Quarrymaster, 1966, p. 4.
20. Wiendl interview, p. 53.
21. William Mulligan, interviewed by the author, May 11, 1995, Woodcliff Lake, New Jersey. Transcript, p. 4.
22. *The Ingersoll-Rand Story.* vol. 4, The Drillmaster, p. 1.
23. *The Ingersoll-Rand Story.* vol. 4, The Crawlmaster, p. 2.
24. William Wearly, interviewed by the author, May 1, 1995, Woodcliff Lake, New Jersey. Transcript, p. 14.
25. Theodore H. Black, interviewed by the author, May 3, 1995, Woodcliff Lake, New Jersey. Transcript, pp. 8-9.

Chapter Eight

1. David C. Garfield, interviewed by the author, December 30, 1994. Transcript, p. 9.

2. C.H. Vivian, *The Ingersoll-Rand Story 1871-1964.* vol. 3, Companies Acquired 1961-1966, 1966, p. 5.

3. D. Wayne Hallstein, interviewed by the author, April 27, 1995, Woodcliff Lake, New Jersey. Transcript, p. 33.

4. James O'Dell, interviewed by the author, May 2, 1995, Woodcliff Lake, New Jersey. Transcript, p. 14.

5. *The Ingersoll-Rand Story.* vol. 3, Companies Acquired 1961-1966, p. 18.

6. *Ibid.,* p. 24.

7. Hallstein interview, p. 34.

8. William Wearly, interviewed by the author, May 1, 1995, Woodcliff Lake, New Jersey. Transcript, p. 40.

9. *The Ingersoll-Rand Story.* vol. 3, Companies Acquired 1961-1966 , p. 27.

10. Wearly interview, p. 5.

11. *Ibid.,* p. 6.

12. *Ibid.,* p. 7.

13. Theodore H. Black, interviewed by the author, May 3, 1995, Woodcliff Lake, New Jersey. Transcript, p. 11.

14. *Ibid.,* p. 12.

15. Wearly interview, p. 8.

16. *Ibid.,* p. 9.

17. Hallstein interview, p. 38.

18. Wearly interview, p. 9.

19. *The Ingersoll-Rand Story.* vol. 3, Companies Acquired 1961-1966, p. 3.

20. Wearly interview, p. 10.

21. *The Ingersoll-Rand Story.* vol. 3, Companies Acquired 1961-1966, pp. 32-33.

22. Dick Johnson, interviewed by the author, November 17, 1994, Woodcliff Lake, New Jersey. Transcript, p. 38.

Chapter Nine

1. William E. Austin, interviewed by the author, November 17, 1994, Woodcliff Lake, New Jersey. Transcript, p. 35.

2. William Wearly, interviewed by the author, May 1, 1995, Woodcliff Lake, New Jersey. Transcript, p. 14.

3. Story by Gene Miller in *G-Rand Times,* published by the G-Men's Association, somewhere in Texas, August 13, 1990, p. 8.

4. Theodore H. Black, interviewed by the author, May 3, 1995, Woodcliff Lake, New Jersey. Transcript, p. 13.

5. Wearly interview, p. 14.

6. *Ibid.,* p. 17.

7. *Ibid.,* 19.

8. Robert Popejoy, interviewed by the author, April 28, 1995. Transcript, p. 2.

9. William Mulligan, interviewed by the author, May 1, 1995, Woodcliff Lake, New Jersey. Transcript, p. 22.

10. Daniel Kletter, interviewed by the author, May 2, 1995, Woodcliff Lake, New Jersey. Transcript, p. 3.

11. C.H. Vivian, *The Ingersoll-Rand Story 1871-1964.* vol. 7, Athens Factory, 1966, p. 1.

12. James O'Dell, interviewed by the author, May 2, 1995, Woodcliff Lake, New Jersey. Transcript, p. 5.

13. David C. Garfield, interviewed by the author, December 20, 1994. Transcript, pp. 32-33.

14. Popejoy interview, p. 7.

15. Mulligan interview, p. 9.

16. *Ibid.,* p. 8.

17. *Ibid.,* p. 13.

18. *The Ingersoll-Rand Story.* vol. 4, The Magnum Drill, p. 1.

19. 1965 *Annual Report,* p. 6.

20. D. Wayne Hallstein, interviewed by the author, April 27, 1995, Woodcliff Lake, New Jersey. Transcript, p. 6.

21. *Ibid.,* p. 8.

22. *Ibid.,* p. 16.

23. *Ibid.,* p. 2.

24. *Ibid.,* p. 38.

25. King Cunningham, interviewed by the author, November 18, 1994, Woodcliff Lake, New Jersey. Transcript, p. 2.

26. *Ibid.,* p. 5.

27. Wearly interview, p. 12.

28. Garfield interview, p. 16.
29. 1967 Annual Report, p. 3.

Chapter Ten

1. Edwin M. Lieberthal, *Progress through Precision. The First 125 years at the Torrington Company.* (The Torrington Company: 1992), p. 30.
2. *Progress through Precision,* p. 57.
3. *Progress through Precision,* p. 58.
4. *Progress through Precision,* p. 72.
5. Al Nixon, interviewed by the author, May 8, 1995, Woodcliff Lake, New Jersey. Transcript, p. 2.
6. William Wearly, interviewed by the author, May 1, 1995, Woodcliff Lake, New Jersey. Transcript, pp. 33ff.
7. 1968 *Annual Report,* p. 4.
8. David C. Garfield, interviewed by the author, December 20, 1994. Transcript, p.21
9. *Ibid.,* pp. 22-23.
10. *Ibid.,* pp. 21-22.
11. J. Frank Travis, interviewed by the author, May 1, 1995, Woodcliff Lake, New Jersey. Transcript, p. 31.
12. Nixon interview, p. 5.
13. *Ibid.*
14. 1985 *Annual Report,* p.26.
15. "Torrington Bearings Drive Automotive Technology," *Ingersoll-Rand World Report,* vol. 2, no. 1, 1987, p. 6.
16. 1994 *Annual Report,* p. 9.
17. Nixon interview, pp. 11-12.
18. Jerry Levine, "Looking Back at how the 'A' Lock was Developed," *Locksmith Ledger,* December 1993, p. 80.
19. Dave Lasier, interviewed by the author, April 26, 1995. Transcript, p. 2.
20. *Memoirs of Charles Kendrick.*
21. *Ibid.,* pp. 77.
22. Lasier interview, p. 9.
23. David C.Garfield, interviewed by the author, December 30, 1994. Transcript, p. 24.
24. Lasier interview, p. 11.
25. *Ibid.*
26. "Schlage helps keep America safe," *Ingersoll-Rand World Report.* vol. 1, no. 3, 1986, p. 8.
27. "Intellis locking system serves lodging industry," *Ingersoll-Rand World Report.* vol. 1, no. 2, 1986, p. 8.
28. Lasier interivew, p. 8.
29. "Chicago White Sox Feel Safe at Home With Door Hardware Group Products," *Ingersoll-Rand World Report.* vol. 6, no. 3, 1991, p. 2.
30. "Schlage Gives 4,000 Locks to Habitat for Humanity," *Ingersoll-Rand World Report.* vol. 10, no. 1, 1995, p. 3.
31. "I Spy," *OnQ, On Quality and Teamwork.* A Managing Total Quality Publication, published by Schlage.

Chapter Eleven

1. William Armstrong, interviewed by the author, May 2, 1995, Woodcliff Lake, New Jersey. Transcript, 2.
2. D. Wayne Hallstein, interviewed by the author, April 27, 1995, Woodcliff Lake, New Jersey. Transcript, p. 14.
3. 1986 *Annual Report to Ingersoll-Rand Shareowners,* p. 8.
4. Hallstein interview, pp. 29-30.
5. William Wearly, interviewed by the author, May 1, 1995, Woodcliff Lake, New Jersey. Transcript, p. 29.
6. Wearly interview, p. 28.
7. Theodore H. Black, interviewed by the author, May 3, 1995, Woodcliff Lake, New Jersey. Transcript, p. 15.
8. Thomas McBride, interviewed by the author, May 1, 1995, Woodcliff Lake, New Jersey. Transcript, p. 2.
9. *Ibid.,* p. 3.
10. *Ibid.,* p. 8.
11. Hallstein interview, p. 5.
12. Wearly interview, p. 42.
13. "Superdrill Rescues 26 Miners Trapped 215 Feet Below Ground," *Ingersoll-*

Rand World Report. vol. 6, no. 3, 1991, p. 6.

14. 1976 *Annual Report,* p. 22.
15. William L. Wearly, chairman, *Remarks before the Stockbrokers Society.* California, November 15 and 16, 1978.

Chapter Twelve

1. John A. Byrne, "...And Then the Bottom Fell Out," *Forbes.* February 14, 1983, pp. 142-144.
2. Thomas McBride, interviewed by the author, May 1, 1995, Woodcliff Lake, New Jersey. Transcript, p. 14.
3. William Wearly, interviewed by the author, May 1, 1995, Woodcliff Lake, New Jersey. Transcript, pp. 31-32.
4. J. Frank Travis, interviewed by the author, May 1, 1995., Woodcliff Lake, New Jersey. Transcript, p. 17.
5. Wearly interview, p. 30.
6. Alexander Massad, interviewed by the author, April 24, 1995. Transcript, p. 1.
7. Steve Taub, "The insurance policy that didn't pay off.," *Financial World.* January 15, 1983, pp. 16-17.
8. McBride interview, p. 18.
9. Skip Remson, interviewed by the author, May 16, 1995. Transcript, p. 7.

10. William J. Armstrong, interviewed by the author, May 2, 1995, Woodcliff Lake, New Jersey. Transcript, p. 4.
11. "Going Where the Customers Are, Worldwide," speech by James E. Perrella at the International Management Seminar, Compagnie de Saint-Gobain, St. Michaels, Maryland, September 11, 1995. Transcript, pp. 8-9.
12. Theodore H. Black, interviewed by the author, May 3, 1995, Woodcliff Lake, New Jersey. Transcript, p. 17.
13. *Ibid,* p. 18.
14. *Ibid.,* p. 19.
15. *Ibid.,* p. 20.
16. *Ibid.,* p. 21.
17. Jay Palmer, "Pumped Up." *Barron's,* June 21, 1993.
18. Steve Doolittle, interviewed by the author, April 26, 1995. Transcript, p. 4.
19. "Ingersoll-Rand demonstrates home air compressors," *Ingersoll-Rand World Report.* vol. 2, no. 2, 1987, p. 3.
20. Daniel Kletter, interviewed by the author, May 2, 1995, Woodcliff Lake, New Jersey. Transcript, p. 9.
21. *Ibid.,* p. 12.
22. *Ibid.*
23. *Ibid.,* p. 16.
24. James Perrella, interviewed by the author,

November 18, 1994, Woodcliff Lake, New Jersey. Transcript, p. 10.
25. "Telemarketing increases customer satisfaction at Air Compressor Group," *Ingersoll-Rand World Report.* vol. 1, no. 3, 1986, p. 6.

Chapter Thirteen

1. James Perrella, interviewed by the author, November 18, 1994, Woodcliff Lake, New Jersey. Transcript, p. 3.
2. James Lahey, interviewed by the author, May 1, 1995, Woodcliff Lake, New Jersey. Transcript, p. 15.
3. *Ibid.,* pp. 5-6.
4. *Ibid.,* p. 8.
5. Perrella interview, p. 5.
6. Stan Orben, interviewed by the author, November 18, 1994, Woodcliff Lake, New Jersey. Transcript, p. 7.
7. Paul Klebnikov, "A traumatic experience." *Forbes,* January 18, 1993.
8. Theodore H. Black, interviewed by the author, May 3, 1995, Woodcliff Lake, New Jersey. Transcript, p. 31.
9. "Ingersoll-Rand Chairman Wins Wall Street Transcript's Gold Award," *Ingersoll- Rand World Report.* vol. 8, no. 1, 1993, p. 6.

10. "Klemm Helps Germans Deal with Buried Toxic Wastes., *Ingersoll-Rand World Report.* vol. 9, no. 2, 1994, p. 8.
11. John Fitzgerald, *speech,* EI-TG Conference, October 18-21, 1992.
12. "Bonneville Dam Lock Project Showcases Range of Ingersoll- Rand Equipment," *Ingersoll-Rand World Report.* vol. 6, no. 3, 1991, p. 4.
13. "Rock Drill Division Introduces New Hydraulic Crawler," *Ingersoll-Rand World Report.* vol. 4, No. 1, 1989, p. 4.

Chapter Fourteen

1. "Ingersoll-Rand Announces Several Acquisitions and Joint Ventures," *Ingersoll- Rand World Report.* vol. 9, no. 2, 1994, p. 2.
2. *Going Where the Customers Are,* speech by James Perrella, at the International Management Seminar, Compagnie de Saint- Gobain, St. Michaels, Maryland, September 11, 1995. Transcript, pp.17-18.
3. Steve Doolittle, interviewed by the author, April 26, 1995. Transcript, p. 4.
4. *Ibid.,* p. 3.
5. *Ibid.,* p. 5.
6. *Ibid.,* p. 6.

7. "Chinese Order Rock Drills for Mammoth Hydroelectric Project," *Ingersoll-Rand World Report."* vol. 9, no. 1, p. 3.
8. Daniel Kletter, interviewed by the author, May 2, 1995, Woodcliff Lake, New Jersey. Transcript, p. 17.
9. Alexander Massad, interviewed by the author, April 24, 1995. Transcript, p. 5.
10. Kletter interview, p. 20.
11. "Going Where the Customers Are, Worldwide," speech by James E. Perrella, at the International Management Seminar, Compagnie de Saint-Gobain, St. Michaels, Maryland, September 11, 1995. Transcript, pp. 14-15.
12. "Ingersoll-Rand and Dresser Industries Propose Worldwide Pump Joint Venture," *Ingersoll-Rand World Report.* vol. 6, no. 2, 1991, p. 2.
13. Theodore H. Black, interviewed by the author, May 3, 1995, Woodcliff Lake, New Jersey. Transcript, p. 24.
14. *Ibid.,* p. 24.
15. Frank Hadfield, interviewed by the author, May 1, 1995, Woodcliff Lake, New Jersey. Transcript, p. 9.
16. *Ibid.,* p. 18.
17. Perrella interview, p. 11

18. 1994 *Annual Report,* p. 10.
19. *Report of 1990 Worldwide Operations,* published by Ingersoll-Rand.
20. Jean Torfs, interviewed by the author, April 28, 1995. Transcript, p. 5.
21. "Ingersoll-Rand prevails in French drilling competition," *Ingersoll-Rand World Report.* vol. 5, no. 1, 1990, p. 2.
22. "Ingersoll-Rand Signs Russian Joint Venture Agreement," *Ingersoll-Rand World Report,* vol. 7, no. 3, 1992, p. 2.
23. Carlo Piva, interviewed by the author, April 27, 1995. Transcript, p. 7.
24. *Ibid.,* p. 8.
25. 1994 *Annual Report,* p. 9.
26. "A Mixture of East and West, Ingersoll-Rand India Forges Ahead," *Ingersoll-Rand World Report,* vol. 7, no. 2, 1992, p. 4.
27. "Cluster Drills Help Develop Interchange Near Saudi Palaces," Ingersoll-Rand World Report, vol. 8, no. 4, 1993, p. 6.
28. "Waterjet Cutting Systems Division Enters European Joint Venture with ABB Robotics," *Ingersoll-Rand World Report,* vol. 6, no. 1, 1991, p. 5.
29. 1994 *Annual Report,* pp. 9-10.
30. "Aided by Compressors, Flying Hospital Treats Blindness in Third World,"

Ingersoll-Rand World Report. vol. 10, no. 1, 1995, p. 8.

Chapter Fifteen

1. "The Unseen Products of Success," an interview with James E. Perrella, *Leaders* magazine, vol. 18, no. 3, July-September 1995.
2. "Scienco Products Protects Farmer Health And Reduces Pesticide Contamination," *Ingersoll-Rand World Report.* vol. 6, no. 3, 1991, p. 5.
3. "NREC Obtains a Navy Contract To Design CFC-free Compressors," *Ingersoll-Rand World Report.* vol. 7, no. 2, 1992, p.8.
4. "Ingersoll-Rand to curb nonhazardous waste generation," *Teamwork,* vol. 12, no. 5, 1994, p. 7.
5. "Pipeline Built with Company Products To Bolster North American Energy Security," *Ingersoll-Rand World Report,* vol. 7, no. 3, 1992, p. 3.
6. "Power Tool Division Designs Products To Improve Assembly Line Conditions," *Ingersoll-Rand World Report.* vol. 6, no. 1, 1991, p.6.
7. "Aro Sanders Deployed to Middle East," *Fast Forward.* April/May 1991.
8. "Technology Helps Aro Win Navy Contract," *Fast Forward.* May/June 1993.
9. "Aro to Relocate European Manufacturing," *Fast Forward.* June/July 1994.
10. "Ingersoll-Rand Acquires Assets of Centri-Spray Corporation," *Ingersoll-Rand World Report.*, vol. 7, no. 2, 1992, p. 9.
11. D. Wayne Hallstein, interviewed by the author, April 27, 1995, Woodcliff Lake, New Jersey. Transcript, p. 18.
12. Theodore H. Black, interviewed by the author, May 3, 1995, Woodcliff Lake, New Jersey. Transcript, p. 32.
13. James Perrella, *speech,* "The Highest Standards: Why Good Ethics is Good Business," for the Executives-In-the-Classroom program, University of Illinois, Chicago, February 8, 1994.
14. Alexander Massad, interviewed by the author, April 24, 1995. Transcript, p. 7.
15. William Armstrong, interviewed by the author, May 2, 1995, Woodcliff Lake, New Jersey. Transcript, p. 5.
16. Al Nixon, interviewed by the author, May 8, 1995, Woodcliff Lake, New Jersey. Transcript, p. 4.
17. Perrella, interviewed by the author, November 18, 1994, Woodcliff Lake, New Jersey. Transcript, p. 13.
18. Perrella, *speech,* "The Highest Standards."
19. *1993 Annual Report,* p. 5.
20. "Ingersoll-Rand Sets New Record For Number of Patents Issued," *Ingersoll-Rand World Report.* vol. 7, no. 1, 1992, p. 3.
21. "The Unseen Products of Success."
22. John Selko, interviewed by the author, April 27, 1995, Woodcliff Lake, New Jersey. Transcript, p. 8.
23. *Ibid.*
24. "R & D Investments Paying Off as Patents Continue Climbing," *Teamwork.* May, 1994, p. 2.
25. Selko interview, p. 3.
26. Selko interview, p. 4.
27. Patricia Nachtigal, interviewed by the author, May 1, 1995, Woodcliff Lake, New Jersey. Transcript, p. 14.
28. "Ingersoll-Rand Plays Important Role in GM's Ambitious Saturn Project," *Ingersoll-Rand World Report.* vol. 6, no. 1, 1991, p. 8.
29. R. Barry Uber, interviewed by the author, May 2, 1995, Woodcliff Lake, New Jersey. Transcript, p. 22.
30. "New Impact Wrench Puts Squeeze on Competition," *Ingersoll-Rand World Report.* vol. 8, no. 1, 1993, p. 8.

31. William Mulligan, interviewed by the author, May 1, 1995, Woodcliff Lake, New Jersey. Transcript, p. 35.

32. Steve Lipin, "Clark Equipment Fights Ingersoll Bid by Filing Civil Suit. *Wall Street Journal,* March 31, 1995.

33. Letter from Perrella to Leo J. McKernan, Chairman, President and Chief Executive Officer of Clark Equipment Company, April 3, 1995.

34. "History of the Clark Equipment Company," Clark Equipment Company, June 1993.

35. Perrella interview, May 1, 1995. Transcript, p. 3.

36. Perrella interview, May 1, 1995. Transcript, p. 3.

37. Perrella, "Remarks to Shareholders," Annual Meeting of Shareholders, Woodcliff Lake, New Jersey, April 27, 1995.

38. Thomas McBride, interviewed by the author, May 1, 1995, Woodcliff Lake, New Jersey. Transcript, p. 21.

39. McBride interview, p. 24.

40. Perrella interview, May 1, 1995, p. 5.

41. Uber interview, p. 16.

42. Perrella interview, May 1995, p. 6.

43. *Ibid.,* p. 8.

44. *Ibid.,* p. 6.

45. Massad interview, p. 2.

46. Uber interview, p. 22.

47. Lahey interview, pp. 22-23.

48. "Torrington-Bedford Wins Ford Q1 Quality Award," *Ingersoll-Rand World Report.* vol. 6, no. 3, 1991, pp. 1-2.

49. Perrella, *speech,* "Changing the Way We Do Things," to the Purchasing and Quality Councils, Charlotte, North Carolina, 10 November 1992. Transcript, 3.

50. Perrella interview, November 18, 1994, p. 14.

51. Perrella, "Remarks to Shareholders."

INDEX